SPONTANEOUS APPRENTICES
Children and Language

The Tree of Life

The Tree of Life

Board of Editors

The Tree of Life

Planned and Edited by RUTH NANDA ANSHEN

SPONTANEOUS APPRENTICES

Children and Language

George A. Miller

A CONTINUUM BOOK

THE SEABURY PRESS · NEW YORK

1977
The Seabury Press
815 Second Avenue
New York, New York 10017

Printed in the United States of America

Library of Congress Cataloging in Publication Data

Miller, George Armitage, 1920–
Spontaneous apprentices.
(The Tree of life) (A Continuum book)
Bibliography: p.
1. Children—Language.   I. Title.   II. Series.
LB1139.L3M56   372.6   77-8677   ISBN 0-8164-9330-8

Contents

The Tree of Life

"Hope deferred maketh the
heart sick,
But when desire cometh, it is a
Tree of Life."
Book of Proverbs 13:12

Inevitably, towards the end of an historical period, when
thought and custom have petrified into rigidity, and
when the elaborate machinery of civilization opposes and
represses man's more noble qualities, life stirs again be-
neath the hard surfaces. Nevertheless, this attempt to define
the purpose of *The Tree of Life* series is set forth with profound trepidation. Man is living through a period of ex-
treme darkness. There is moral atrophy, an internal destruc-
tive radiation within us as the result of the collapse of values hitherto cherished—but now betrayed. We seem to be
face to face with an apocalyptic destiny. The anomie, the
chaos, surrounding us is causing almost a lethal disintegra-
tion of the person as well as ecological and demographic
disaster. Our situation is indeed desperate. And there is no
glossing over the deeper and unresolved tragedy with
which our lives are filled. Science itself as now practised
tells us what *is*, but not what *ought* to be; *de*scribing but not
*pre*scribing.

And yet, we cannot say "yes" to our human predicament.
The Promethean protest must not be silenced by lame sub-
mission. We have been thrown into this indifferent universe, and although we cannot change its structure, we can
temporarily, for our own lifetime and for the life of the
human race, build shelters of meaning, of empathy and
compassion. Thus, for the fleeting moment that our lives

fill, we can rise above time and indifferent eternity, struggling for the ray of light that pierces through this darkness. We can transcend the indifference of nature or, to be blasphemous, this badly messed up creation, and listen to the "still, small voice"—the source of hope without which there would be no humanity at all. For in this way, we can again reaffirm the glory of the human spirit.

This series is dedicated to that kind of understanding which may be compared with the way birds understand the singing of other birds. We, as men, women and children, need to learn to understand and respect each other, beyond exploitation, beyond self-interest, and to experience what it means *to be* by discovering, if we can, the secret of life.

My introduction to *The Tree of Life* is not, of course, to be construed as a prefatory essay to each individual volume. These few pages simply endeavor to set forth the general aim and purpose of this series as a whole. This statement hopefully may serve the reader with a new orientation in his thinking, more specifically defined by those scholars who have been invited to participate in this intellectual, spiritual and moral endeavor so desperately needed in our time, and who recognize the relevance of that non-discursive experience of life which the discursive, analytical, method alone is unable to convey.

The Tree of Life has summoned the world's most concerned thinkers to rediscover the experience of *feeling* as well as of thought. Such is the difference between the Tree of Life and the Tree of Knowledge. The Tree of Life presides over the coming of the possible fulfillment of self-awareness—not the isolated, alienated self, but rather the participation in the life-process with other lives and other forms of life. It is a cosmic force and may possess liberating powers of allowing man to become what he is.

The further aim of this series is certainly not, nor could it be, to disparage knowledge or science. The authors themselves in this effort are adequate witness to this fact. Actually, in viewing the role of science, one arrives at a much more modest judgment of the role which it plays in our whole body of knowledge. Original knowledge was probably not acquired by us in the active sense; most of it must have been given to us in the same mysterious way as, and perhaps as part of, our consciousness. As to content and usefulness, scientific knowledge is an infinitesimal fraction of natural knowledge. However, it is a knowledge, the structure of which is endowed with beauty because its abstractions satisfy our urge for specific knowledge much more fully than does natural knowledge itself, and we are justly proud of it because we can call it our own creation. It teaches us clear thinking and the extent to which clear thinking helps us to order our sensations it is a marvel which fills the mind with ever new and increasing admiration and awe. But science must now begin to include the realm of human values, lest even the memory of what it means to be human be forgotten.

It is also the aim of *The Tree of Life* to present solid analyses of the critical issues of our time which, though resting on an intuitively conceived basis, are scholarly productions in the true sense of the word. And although there is a concern with the non-discursive element of all knowledge, the fruits the scholars in this Series hope to gather will be an expansion of such knowledge, open to verification and experience. For we are living in an emergency situation which requires approaches with practical consequences. And these consequences are not confined to the realm of political action; they refer as much to a reformation of science and education as to a renewal of ethics and human attitudes and behavior.

The gap between religion and science has been largely eliminated by modern advances in our concepts of cosmology, the nature of matter, the forces that move the universe and created life and the nature of mind and the mind-brain relation. Therefore science indeed, if not misused, becomes extremely relevant and must admit into its orbit revelation, faith and intuition.

A new dimension has now in the latter half of this twentieth century appeared in our consciousness in spite of the tyranny of our technocratic society. We yearn to *experience* that kind of intuition of a reality which allows us to remember that we are *human*. And this consciousness of what it means to be human is an all-pervading command which our nature summons us to respect everywhere: in science, in philosophy, commerce, revolution, religion, art, sanctity and even in error which needs to be transformed, when the heart and mind of humankind attain a certain depth of mastery in the power of discovering new horizons and taking great risks.

Self-awareness is an incomparable spiritual gain since it begets *life* unencumbered by excessive intellectual baggage. The Tree of Knowledge, important and fruitful in itself, is no substitute for the Tree of Life, the fruits of which Adam and Eve did not eat in the primordial garden. Now we are, so to speak, given a second chance since the Tree of Life and the Tree of Knowledge have one and the same root. Self-awareness then becomes actual. The question is, however, how the conditions may be provided. This is a matter of the interplay of freedom and destiny.

The question pursued in the many respective disciplines expressed through the invited scholars, is how the actualization of the *experience of life,* not merely the idea about life, may be achieved through the fulfillment of the potentialities in each one of us. In order to answer this question, we must consider, as this series tries to do, the dynamics of life, and the historical dimensions in an anticipatory way so that the goal always remains in the path. This last and all-embracing dimension of life comes to its full realization in man as an aspect of the universe and of matter itself. Man is the bearer of the spirit when the conditions for its realization are present.

We bow to the *life force,* to that mysterious energy which creates life. The observation of a particular potentiality of being, whether it is that of another species or of a person, actualizing themselves in time and space, has led to the concept of *life,* life as the actuality of being. A tension is always present between matter and form in all existence. If the actualization of the potential is a structural condition of all beings, and if this actualization is called "life," then the universal concept of life, in all its manifold expressions among all species and not only in mankind, becomes unavoidable. Thus *The Tree of Life* endeavors to define the *multidimensionality of all life,* the inorganic with its mystery as well as the organic with its mastery, the psychological, historical and the spiritual. Such is the "alchemy" of life. Such is the immediate experience of the *consciousness* of life, of *living life itself.* Such is the new threshold on which we stand.

Newton would have despaired if he could have envisaged the duality of the universe to which his work was to lead, and to the determinism which so completely eroded the Aristotelian view of purpose. It seems to be our good fortune that the recent discoveries in science have themselves, in turn, undermined the possibility of belief in a universe contingent only on those aspects of nature which can be revealed by science alone. Could it be that the world is approaching a remarkable synthesis of the disparate issues in science and religion which have been such an obstacle in this generation?

Emphasis in Western culture has been placed, for the greater part, on knowledge which too often has degenerated into quantitative information. The fact that probability and certainty, faith and knowledge, require intuition has frequently been ignored while the data of observation, requiring only the act of observing with one's physical eyes, exclusive of the creative process of intuition, of envisaging, have been extolled as primary in human consciousness, and have been accepted as more important than the experience of life itself.

Anthropocentric values superimposed on all life—whether organic or inorganic—are evidences of a form of power incompatible with the reality of the multidimensionality of living creatures in whatever animal, entomological, even perhaps cosmological and human forms *life* may manifest itself. There is no justification for enforcing the concept of causality on the entire universe as the only possible form of relationship. In particular, while many phenomena exhibited by living beings can be foreseen on the basis of causal relations with the past, we should be aware of the possibility of relations of another type, for example, the circularity of reason and consequences in addition to the linearity of cause and effect.

There is abundant anthropological evidence that supports

the intuitive perspective of the experience of life and life processes and indicates that our implicit knowledge of phenomena may be as old as humanity itself. And we can now begin to use this knowledge as a regular part of our scientific understanding of consciousness.

The Tree of Life, a series of volumes on a variety of vital problems and written by the most concerned thinkers of our time, attempts to show the structural kinship of life and knowledge and to overcome the false dualism which indeed has never existed, since unity and reality are one.

We are faced with planning and with choice. We can change the course of human life. What do we want to do with this newly achieved power? What is to become of the freedom of the individual in a genetically, politically, and socially engineered society? The implications of genetic engineering are especially serious and we have now reached the time when we must ask ourselves: Even though some things are possible, are they desirable? The centers of economic and even political power become less and less national, and the state and its corporations are powers, not institutions serving the people. The spirit has petrified in the lava of phenomena.

We cannot know where our new knowledge of life will lead us. Our fate, as the fate of the world, or the cosmos, is not fixed. All this depends on chance, freedom, will, and purpose. Life itself is a struggle against randomness. It strives to replace randomness by arrangements which give some aesthetic satisfaction and which may have some meaning. And even if we, as humanity, in coming generations of greater longevity, do indeed endure, it will require a wealth of further complexity and organization. Perhaps the earth itself—and even some galaxies—and mankind as well, will some day disappear, by accident, inability of adaptation and mutation, or the universe's power of depleting itself. Yet our consciousness and the values locked up in it are now entrusted to us, waiting for our decision for a life lived, not as a fragment of knowledge or information alone, but as an active element of experience.

Turning our backs for a moment on the vast cosmic challenges which confront man in his perceptions of the cosmology of life, and looking into ourselves for an elementary analysis and understanding of our intuitive conception of past and present, we find it to be essentially based on two facts. First, our need to accept at all times a single, unitary structure forever present in spite of its complexity. For in any sequence of states of consciousness we may live through, each is simultaneous with the whole in all its parts. Second, the fact of memory, by which we can embrace in our present consciousness elements of a previous state of being (what Plato called *anamnesis,* or spiritual recollection of other lives lived in each of us before our present life). Thus we recognize, if only at times dimly or subconsciously, that there is the same simultaneity in unbroken continuity of past, present, and future and manifesting itself as fresh, current happenings. We compare these vestiges of the past with the facts of the present and derive therefrom our notion of the passage of time.

Confronted by the difficulties of finding a physical interpretation of the temporal characteristics of consciousness, we may assume one or another of two distinct attitudes. The first, which should be called defeatist, is to divide once and for all the universe into two separate parts: the world of mind and the world of matter. This means of course completely abandoning the effort to grasp and understand the whole, or life itself. The other attitude is to use any new notions—such as those derived recently from microphysics, psychology, and biology—in an effort to move toward the basic unity of matter and mind, to reconcile the present unity of consciousness not only with the chain of causation but with the mystery of life itself. The erroneous "gap" between matter and mind has been artificially postulated by man in order to facilitate the analysis of their parts.

It is suggested that the mystical Tree of Life is at the same time the tree of transcendent authority—as distinct from mere power. Each branch of this tree has a common root at times unknown and even unknowable in a logical sense. It can be intuited and experienced since it is not only the root of all roots, it is also the sap of the Tree. Every branch represents an attribute and exists by virtue of the hidden transcendent authority inherent in it. And this

Tree of Life is the substance of the universe. It grows throughout the whole of creation and spreads its branches through all its ramifications. Thus, all mundane and created things exist only because something of the authority of the Tree of Life lives and acts through them. The body and the soul, though different in nature—one being material, the other spiritual—nevertheless constitute an organic whole and are *substantially* the same. The conception of life as an organism has the advantage of answering the question why there are different manifestations of the transcendent quality of life itself. For is not the organic life of the spirit one and the same, although, for example, the function of the hands differs from that of the eyes? The universe is in man as man is in the universe.

We have forgotten that throughout antiquity, down to the advent of the experimental sciences, every movement or change in the outside world had a direct bearing on man. Since human affairs were linked by an interlocking system of correspondence—with the planets, the animal world, the four elements—nothing that occurred in the macrocosm but that it had some impact upon them. This tangled network of interrelationships and concordances collapsed by virtue of the discoveries of mechanics in the universe by Copernicus, Galileo, Newton, and Einstein; only the movement of objects and the laws that govern them were considered important and relevant to reality. Man himself was forgotten. Whether these laws of mechanics concern planets or molecules, these movements and laws were considered no longer directly related to the complicated events that together make up the major portion of our daily lives.

Hand in hand with this dehumanization of man and the world, a profound transformation of its laws took place, giving birth to a new conception of causality. The universe assumed a continuous geometrical structure in which there was no place for individual beings, human or animal. While this kind of revolutionary view of reality managed for a long time to satisfy the demands of experimental science, it administered a profound shock to all of us who remained attached to the basic truth, the beliefs and hypotheses which are in themselves totalities.

The scientific world, as we have inherited it, with all its plethora of information, its technology, does not present a picture of the real world and of man in it. It gives us an abundance of factual information, puts all our data in a magnificently consistent order, but it remains ominously silent about all that is really near to our hearts, all that really matters to a lived life. It cannot tell us anything about red and blue, bitter and sweet, physical pain and physical delight; it knows nothing of what is beautiful and ugly, good and evil, joy and sorrow, the infinite and the finite. Within the scientific world-picture, all these experiences take care of themselves; they are amply accounted for by direct, energetic interplay. Even the human body's movements are its own. The scientific-technological interpretation of man and the world allows us to imagine the total display as that of a mechanical clockwork which ticks away without there being any consciousness, will, freedom, justice, memory, tragedy, endeavor, pain, delight, tears, laughter, sacrifice, moral responsibility, aesthetic experience or religious insight. Man has been relegated, he is expendable, evaporated in this scientific-technological world-structure.

The philosopher, seeking the essence of life, is confronted with the desperate drive to discover some basis, some anti-mechanism, since his entire experience of vital feelings and function, his intrinsic values, warn him against a deterministic and mechanical image which is spurious. For our problem seems to be therefore that every scientist is constantly faced with the objective description of data by which we understand communication in unambiguous terms. But how can objectivity of description be retained during the growth of experience within and beyond daily life occurrences? The widening of the conceptual framework has not only served to restore order within the respective branches of knowledge, but has also disclosed analogies in the analysis and synthesis of *experience* in apparently separated domains of knowledge, suggesting the possibility of an ever more embracing insight into the nature of life itself. Yet, life is not isomorphic with knowledge. Life draws us far beyond knowledge and happily transcends it. And when this truth is realized, then the system of scientific knowledge may be made the vehicle for the actualization of new emotions. The fact of consciousness as applied to ourselves as well as to others is indispensable when dealing with the human situation. In view of this, one may well wonder how materialism and determinism—the doctrine that life could be explained by sophisticated combinations of physical and chemical laws—could have for so long been accepted by the majority of scientists. Obviously there is something in nature, in the nature of man, that transcends matter. For now nature, it is suggested, may be on the point of being disenthralled from the deterministic demon; and although the assertion of determinism is certainly possible, it is by no means necessary, and when examined closely, is not even practicable.

Therefore, the authors in *The Tree of Life* summon us to ask the question: What does it mean to be human? Why do we feel, as we indeed do, at least some of us, that there is no break in the laws of continuity applicable to the universe as to man? For the present is filled with the past and pregnant with the future. And we now must realize that the finite is akin to the infinite, as man is akin to eternity, and that this kinship allows him like the transcendent demiurge to fashion the world, and that the performance of this task is the truly human obligation. This constitutes the present profound change in man's consciousness. The fruit he has eaten from the Tree of Life has carved out for him a difficult but rewarding path: a revolt against traditionally accepted scientific principles and a yearning for that qualitative metamorphosis in which the new stage of consciousness comes into existence as the result of a decisive jolt and is characteristic of a life of the spirit which, when coupled with the organic development, is like the planting of a seed whose successive unfolding has given man the nourishing fruit of the Tree of Life, for man's organism is instinct with the drive toward primal unity.

Man is capable of making the world what it is destined to be: a community of people who have the resources of each particular region in common and who share in the goods and cultures and knowledge, a task far from being completed. We are faced with a serious problem, since the wavelength of change is shorter than the lifespan of man and the time required for adaptation and mutation is limited. Life itself is threatened. Not only must we continue to emphasize the pressing problems and immediate needs, not only as a goal but as a solution, to recognize the indissoluble union between progress and that of liberty, virtue, and respect for the natural rights of man, but also the effects of life on the destruction of prejudice.

The volumes in *The Tree of Life* endeavor to emphasize the pulse of the present and its meaning for the future. The past is with us. The present summons us. Our sociological theories, our political economy, our scientific potentialities and achievements, our religious and metaphysical principles and our doctrines of education are derived from an unbroken tradition of great thinkers and of practical examples from the age of Plato in the fifth century B.C. to the end of the last century. The whole tradition is warped by the vicious assumption that each generation should substantially live amid the conditions governing the lives of its fathers and should transmit those conditions to mold with equal force the lives of their children. *We are now living in the first period of human history for which this assumption is false.*

Other subjects to be explored by the invited authors are problems of communications media which must awaken to their responsibility and to be conducted by men and women who bring not only method but substance; in other words, *live* explorations into all problems of contemporary society in the East and the West, and who will not be automatic, static products of an established social culture. It is the permanent "energy" of that which is essentially *man* which must be transmitted from one generation to another, thereby giving criteria to judgments and actions so that the continuity of human life and the evolutionary force which is *mind* may be preserved. Thus we maintain an openness to the coexistence of all qualities that characterizes the living world.

No individual destiny can be separated from the destiny of the universe. Whitehead has stated the doctrine that every event, every step or process in the universe involves both effects from past situations and the anticipation of future potentialities. Basic for this doctrine is the assumption that the course of the universe results from a multiple and never ending complex of steps developing out of one another. Thus in spite of all evidence to the contrary, we conclude that there is a continuing and permanent energy of that which is not only man but all of life itself. And it is for this reason that we espouse life. For not an atom stirs in matter, organic and inorganic, that does not have its cunning duplicate in Mind. And faith in *life* creates its own verification.

Ruth Nanda Anshen
New York

I am indebted and grateful to Professor Chiang Yee for calling my attention to the Chinese ideograph, meaning *LIFE* (the fourth century B.C.) which is used on the jacket and binding of the volumes in *The Tree of Life* as its colophon.

R.N.A.

For my Mother
who was interested
in children before I was.

Preface

It is a common idea, one often featured in introductory textbooks, that science advances by an iterative process of formulating and testing hypotheses. There must be some truth to it. If you examine a typical article in some journal of experimental science, you will find a standard sequence used for expository purposes: first, a statement of the problem, including references to scientific knowledge already accumulated and the author's hypothesis; second, a description of the method used to test that hypothesis; third, an account of the results of the test; finally, a discussion relating those results to the initial hypothesis. The true hypotheses are collected and eventually published in books, which, when assembled on the shelves of a library, constitute the accumulated body of scientific knowledge.

This picture of science is misleading in many respects, however. The most obvious omission is the experiment that failed and was never published. And, as some critics of this view have pointed out, even when an experiment succeeds the hypothesis that accounts so neatly for the published observations was, more often than not, arrived at after the observations were made; the faulty hunch that led to the experiment in the first place is silently relegated to an appropriate limbo. Moreover, the situation that made it necessary to adopt one method of experimentation rather than some other is seldom explained. The first-hand feel of research in this area is taken for granted. The talent for being surprised at the right moment is underplayed. The important role of serendipity is minimized. And the fact that the knowledge accumulated in a scientist's head is more important in determining the course of science than is the knowledge accumulated in his library is seldom mentioned. Those who believe that science is so important to modern industrialized society that we should make every effort to understand it and its practitioners as accurately and objectively as possible, have frequently deplored scientists' efforts to present their work as an inevitable march forward from rational insight to established truth.

In the case of certain truly significant advances, historians of science have been at some pains to reconstruct what actually went on behind the journal articles. Their accounts necessarily involve a whole range of untold failures, accidents, personal triumphs, and, above all, a reconstruction of what it was like to think in a certain way before the advance occurred. From their work a nonscientist can gain a better understanding of science as a human enterprise. But such reconstructions require intensive work that can be justified only by the great significance of the events involved. If that were the only view one had of the scientific process, it would seem a constant round of mind-shattering revolutions.

This book was written in the belief that there is a place for accounts of the human side of "insignificant" science as well. In the sense intended here, most scientific work is insignificant. Science is a large edifice built from stones and timbers put in place by many workers. If "significant" is reserved for those rare occasions on which a bay window is suddenly transformed into a new wing, then most of the construction work is not significant in that sense. Most scientific work is neither an inevitable march forward into truth nor a constant turmoil of revolutionary upheavals. It is hard work, carried on with normal human passions and confusions, intended to reduce the number of alternative views of the universe and its inhabitants that a rational person might subscribe to. Surely there must be some interest in such experience, even when the results are, by popular standards, insignificant.

To preface this book with weighty questions about the

nature of science may be a bit misleading. One reason for raising them here is that they are little explored in the pages that follow, yet they provided much of the motivation for writing the book. The weight is lightened in the actual telling by the fact that the science in question is psychology. In the final analysis, science can study only three things: matter, life, and mind. Of the three, mind is the most intriguing, albeit the most difficult, and scientific progress has not yet succeeded in moving this fascinating subject beyond the comprehension of the average person. Because the science considered here is psychology, the more general message that the book is intended to convey could be obscured.

Psychology is hardly a prototype of science. Some would deny that it is a science at all, but many psychologists think they are scientists, and I am one of those. The story I have to tell, however, may not be representative of insignificant science in general. If I can tell it well, perhaps some mute, inglorious Newtons in more established fields will tell more representative tales. I do not believe it is unrepresentative, however. Insignificant, yes, but if it were unrepresentative it would not be worth telling.

It will be necessary to introduce some psychological ideas in order to tell the story, but the intent is not to report new scientific findings or to promote a new theory of the mind. The intent is to reveal how my friends and I worked on a research problem for two years and why we did what we did and failed to do what we neglected. I believe the matrix in which that activity went on was representative of conditions under which science develops in many fields other than psychology.

The particular problem we worked on was the growth of vocabulary in young children. Why we chose that problem, how we interpreted and extended it, what we did, and what we think we learned about it provide narrative threads for the following pages; I will not try to offer a summary statement here. It should be obvious, however, that how children learn words is a complicated process, related closely to how they learn about the things they talk about—understanding vocabulary growth is a small but important part of the larger problem of understanding cognitive development in general. And it should also be obvious that the children who did the learning must play an important role in my story. Since children are intrinsically interesting people, they, too, help to lighten and humanize this account of our scientific efforts. But it is our group efforts to investigate this problem that will hold the center of the stage. I have not attempted a technical summary of the results—the work is continuing even as I write, and will eventually be reported in detail in scientific journals and texts for those who share our research interests. And I have not attempted a guidebook on cognitive development for parents and teachers. Future authors of such books may find here some useful footnotes, but the scope of our investigations was too narrow to provide an adequate foundation for a general manual on the growth of the mind.

Science is a way of gathering knowledge, and therefore I hope it is not inappropriate to present the story autobiographically, as an episode in a life devoted largely to self-education, to the gathering of knowledge for personal satisfaction. I have never been sufficiently clear about the difference and probably have often rationalized the personal satisfaction of my curiosity in the more socially approved language of scientific progress. But I suspect that that, too, is not unrepresentative of people in my position.

I have had to rely at many points on my personal memories and interpretations of events that others may remember somewhat differently. No doubt I have viewed my own contributions in a more favorable light than they deserve; I cannot hope to be atypical in that respect either. Where possible, I have consulted written records in my files— reports, correspondence, appointment calendars, memoranda, grant applications, and the like—and where those sources failed I have appealed to my colleagues for their personal recollections. I am indebted to Mark and Mary Jo Altom, Susan Carey, Michael Cole, Madeleine Dobriner, John Dore, Peter Kranz, Donna Lyons, Katherine Miller, Keith Stenning, and especially to Elsa Bartlett and Joyce Weil for corroborating, correcting, and supplementing my initial account, but of course I alone am responsible for any faulty interpretations or errors of fact that may have eluded their efforts. It is my personal view of what went on that is presented here, not a group consensus. I am concerned that it be as true as possible, but I am even more concerned that it be candid. And candor is a personal matter. I am also indebted to Ruth Nanda Anshen, Eric Wanner, and Stephen White who were kind enough to give me good advice from the point of view of nonparticipants.

The title I have chosen is intended to acknowledge the story's true heroes, the children whose growing mastery of language we attempted to understand. It is linked in my mind with the French *apprentissage,* which has become a more general term for the learning process than "apprentice" might normally imply—as in Henri Grégoire's *L'Apprentissage du Langage,* for example. Young children have an unusual faculty for learning language and it is well that they do, for we expect them to learn far more than we could self-consciously teach them. In order to learn it, they must become apprentices. This apprenticeship they accept spontaneously and with enthusiasm, in a spirit of learning all too rare in more formal educational situations. Adult learners are often too afraid of being childish to allow themselves to be childlike. If any deeper wisdom can be garnered from a study of children's language learning, it would probably be how to learn as a spontaneous apprentice, for even serious scientists are apprentices to nature.

Teacher (to group):   Do you know who that man was?

Girl: Who?

Teacher: That was Doctor Miller.

Girl: Who's that?

Teacher: This is his school.

Girl: I went to this. This is MY school.

Teacher: Yeah.

Girl: It is.

Teacher: Well, he's the man who got the money to open this school.

Boy: Is this my school?

Teacher: Sure!

Girl: It's MY school too.

On Founding Schools
and Other Personal Matters

"Start, start right here."
Jeff

In 1972 I opened a postgraduate School of Developmental Psychology and enrolled myself as the only student. Such measures are often necessary when you are too old (or too proud) to be admitted to anyone else's school and you decide to master a new field of knowledge. Unfortunately, some who would like to pursue such a course are intimidated by their own institutional conceptions. Buildings. Faculty. Students. Laboratories. Library. Endowment. How can you assemble all that?

It is surprisingly easy. I do it all the time. For buildings, a comfortable hat will serve nicely; few janitorial services are required. The faculty is easiest of all. A dream faculty for developmental psychology might include G. Stanley Hall, Alfred Binet, William Stern, Heinz Werner, Sigmund and Anna Freud, Erik Erikson, Jean Piaget, Nancy Bayley, Jerome Bruner, Roger Brown. Never mind that you cannot afford the salaries of such people—some of them are dead. Their ideas are all you want and the best of those have been carefully preserved in their books and articles. You can learn more in an hour reading than two hours listening to them. In my school I supplemented these distinguished people with a junior faculty who taught me even more: some three-year-old children.

For students I had myself. That sounds lonely, but the absurdly low tuition more than offsets the solitude. For laboratories, the whole world lies at a psychologist's doorstep. Because I happen to be in an unusually advantaged position, I made a mistake about my own laboratory. In 1973 I actually started one that included a nursery school for the three-year-olds who served as faculty in my private School of Developmental Psychology—but more about that later. For a library, you can buy a few of the most important books and, if a university library is not open to you, most public libraries are warmly accommodating. The endowment can be a bit sticky. Let me assume that you already have the major component, an active and curious mind. Beyond that you need time, privacy, and enough money to live on.

The principle that you will starve if you do not eat applies democratically to rich and poor alike, but that fact has never comforted the poor. The problem has plagued scholarship throughout recorded history. The best solution is to be rich. Lacking that, next best is to have a rich patron. Economic statistics being what they are, most of us must rely on patrons: parents, philanthropists, welfare checks, a working spouse. My patron is The Rockefeller University, in New York, which pays me a generous salary in return for which I am expected to do—my best. I try hard to meet that expectation, my efforts being interrupted only by occasional periods devoted to fitting gratitude for the life I have been chosen to lead. Unfortunately, however, my experience has given me little wisdom to share on the art of attracting patrons. If you are less favored, perhaps you could still found a *small* school?

In any case, in the spring of 1975 I flunked myself out and closed my personal School of Developmental Psychology. My trouble was with the junior faculty. I simply could not predict what they were going to say. Like most adults, I was insufficiently innocent, a condition widely known to be incurable. Further study only exacerbates it. (I also closed the laboratory school for the children, but there were other reasons for that.)

It was somewhat perverse of me to open my personal school at that particular time; for years I had deliberately avoided other people's children. At Harvard University around 1960 I stumbled into an enormously fruitful collaboration with J. S. Bruner in an enterprise we called, somewhat imperiously, the Center for Cognitive Studies. In those days "cognition" was considered a naughty word by most scientific psychologists; under the sway of behaviorism, all mentalistic terms were on a par with phlogiston. But Jerry Bruner proudly nailed it to the door that Dean McGeorge Bundy gave us and, with the further patronage of John Gardner, then president of the Carnegie Foundation of New York, we set about making it respectable. Bruner had been working to that end for several years, and his own line of research had led him to study younger and younger people. My contribution was to study the psychology of language, a form of knowledge that now seems to me so indubitably cognitive that I still marvel that it took Noam Chomsky to teach me not to mumble when I said so. You would think that, if I really wanted to understand children, then would have been the time to open my personal School of Developmental Psychology. But we had a comfortable division of labor, children for Bruner and sentences for Miller; nothing but trouble could have come from my moving into his backyard.

As I recall it now, Bruner and I hoped the center would be guided by a troika, the third horse being Roger Brown. Brown is a social psychologist best known for his studies of child language; he could have filled to overflowing the obvious gap between us. But Brown is not a joiner and we had to settle for his blessings. The intersection between Bruner's children and Miller's language was occupied, therefore, by several younger people, the most important in my intellectual life being David McNeill, who had come to Harvard to work with Roger Brown. Somewhere around 1965 McNeill and I agreed to write a chapter on psycholinguistics for *The Handbook of Social Psychology;* we also taught a course together and cooperated in various conferences. In all of these joint enterprises I adhered to my fixed division of labor: McNeill worried about child language and I worried about adult language. It would have been so easy to learn about children then, but efficiency dictated otherwise.

Even Noam Chomsky, on whom I have relied for what little I know about the theory of language, was interested in how children learn to talk. He tried to imagine a language acquisition system that would take a large corpus of utterances as input and produce as output the grammatical rules of the language. His point was that any device capable of such a feat would have to be designed by nature to ignore many plausible but incorrect hypotheses. Chomsky's emphasis on the hereditary basis of man's faculty for language strongly influenced both McNeill and me, but McNeill went on to develop a theory of language acquisition based on those ideas and I did not.

In 1967 I left Harvard for Rockefeller, and Thomas G. Bever accompanied me. Bever is a psychologist at heart, but his doctoral work was done in linguistics under Chomsky. At Rockefeller he and I fell into my well established pattern: he became interested in child language and I pursued everything else. Shortly thereafter Michael Cole, also interested in children, joined the Rockefeller faculty. But still I felt no urge to enroll myself in Developmental Psychology.

For more than a decade I worked closely with people who could have taught me a great deal about children and how they learn their first language. And I have not even mentioned the graduate students whose doctoral work on child language I helped to supervise. I suppose I did not get actively involved because I did not have to. Someone else near at hand was always more eager to pursue that approach.

From 1967 to 1970 I allowed myself to become too involved in science policy at the national level. Between the American Psychological Association, the National Institutes of Health, the National Academy of Sciences, and task forces of the President's Scientific Advisory Committee, I was working about half-time in Washington. Sitting at committee meetings with the great and near great was heady stuff, but while it inflated my ego it also deflated my competence as a working scientist. Life is a series of games in which the reward for winning at one game is the privilege of playing a different game. Seldom was the specialized knowledge I had used to win the game of experimental psychology of any value in playing the committee game. By the time I realized that my trips to Washington were not really satisfying, I was in serious need of intellectual retreading.

In 1970, therefore, I took two years away from Rockefeller

as a member of the Institute for Advanced Study in Princeton, New Jersey. At the Institute I was at last isolated from child watchers. I was free to plunge sixteen hours a day into whatever I chose. And I was in an inner state of despair bordering on panic. My head seemed totally empty. As I tried to pick up the threads of my intellectual life, I began to think about verbs of motion. It was pure accident. On my instructions, a research assistant had conducted a study of people's judgments of the similarity of meaning among a few motion verbs (*walk, run, stroll, swim, jog, trot,* and so on) and the results had been exactly the opposite of what I had expected. I arrived in Princeton with those data in a box and, having nothing better to do, began trying to construct an explanation. I soon decided that it would be impossible to understand how people relate these particular verbs to one another until I knew more generally what the semantic components are of all the motion verbs in English. So I settled down with a dictionary, drew up a list of more than 200 motion verbs, and tried to classify them in some sensible way. It became deeply engrossing. The patterns were subtle and beautiful. I wrote a paper about them. I had no clear view of where I was going, but I was going somewhere. The feeling of panic began to recede.

In 1971 Philip N. Johnson-Laird came to the Institute for a year's leave of absence from the University of London. He read my work, liked it, and we decided to collaborate on a short paper pointing out the heavy perceptual contribution to the semantic components I had isolated. Since the relation between language and perception is one of the oldest and most tortured subjects in the history of western thought, our short paper rapidly grew into a large and ambitious book about how lexical knowledge might be organized in a person's memory. By then I was avidly reading everything I could find on semantic analysis and my rebirth as a working psychologist seemed well assured. The task absorbed my best energies until it appeared as *Language and Perception* some five years later.

Language and Perception is a highly theoretical account and as it grew we both became restless to test it. We could think of four lines that might be followed. One was to collect the subjective judgments and measure the reaction times of adult speakers of English when they are asked to respond to various relations between words. That approach was being actively pursued by many psychologists whose work we reviewed in the book; we both wanted to supplement that work with other kinds of tests. A second possibility was to try to instantiate our theoretical notions in computer programs that could simulate some of the lexical processes we described. Johnson-Laird favored that approach and that, following my policy of divide and conquer, left the other two for me. The third was to test our ideas, which grew out of intuitions about English, on languages outside the familiar Indo-European family. If what we were saying had psychological validity, it should hold for speakers of other languages. Unfortunately, learning one or more exotic languages sufficiently well to have reliable intuitions about semantic relations between words in them is not a task that someone over fifty can undertake with any confidence of success. So that left the fourth approach.

The fourth way to test our ideas was to watch lexical knowledge develop in children. Any study of development depends heavily on one's conception of what is developing. The study of lexical development had lagged behind the study of grammatical development, largely because Chomsky had given us a clearer picture of what was developing grammatically. We thought that we could now redress the balance. We claimed to know what must be developing lexically; what was more natural than to be the first to exploit those ideas? By this time, however, all my former collaborators who knew something about this approach had gone on to higher things. I would have to do it myself, but I knew how little of their competence had rubbed off on me over the years.

In preparation, I began looking at the more accessible studies of the growth of vocabulary in children. It struck me that they were of two kinds. There were the parental diaries in which a child's utterances are faithfully recorded over an extended period of time. Typically, these longitudinal studies ended at just the point where I became most interested: when the child's vocabulary began to grow so rapidly that the parents could no longer keep track of it. The other kind of study was cross-sectional: vocabulary tests were given to different groups of children at different ages. The results made it possible to estimate how many words an average child knows as a function of his age, but they provided little insight into how any particular word is learned. I began to think about longitudinal studies that did not try to keep track of all the words a child knows, but concentrated on particular groups of words about which Johnson-Laird and I had explicit semantic hypotheses. I convinced myself that those were the kinds of data I needed, but I had only the vaguest idea how to collect them. I had a lot to learn.

That is why, in the fall of 1972, I opened my personal postgraduate School of Developmental Psychology and enrolled as a student. By the spring of 1975 I recognized that, whatever the real reason for the lag in our under-standing of lexical development, it was not attributable to the lack of an explicit theory of what was developing.

At that point I retired to consider what had gone wrong. It was not the theory. The theory may be wrong, for all I know, but that was not what my study of developmental psychology had told me. My real problem was that it seemed so difficult to get inside children's heads and see the world and language through their eyes. On that score our semantic analyses are totally silent.

The Best Laid Plans

"I want to, I want to . . .
[inaudible]"
Vanessa

A person willing to say "That is vacuous crap" whenever he smells the breaking of intellectual wind will make some enemies, but in the competitive world of academia he will also gather many rewards. So many, in fact, that such denunciations are probably made more often than they are deserved, particularly by novitiates. With so much to read and study, any basis for winnowing may be too quickly accepted. In dismissing something on these grounds, however, you must be careful in selecting your authority; some will say it about anything they do not understand. Pick an authority who has earned the right to say it. And be especially cautious when the authority is yourself.

Once, early in my efforts to educate George Miller, I undertook to read an introductory textbook in sociology. (That was before I knew that you should read original sources by the masters in any field; most textbooks are useful only to help you discover who the masters are.) All I recall of it now is page after dreary page devoted to developing a definition of a social group, a term whose meaning I felt was already sufficiently clear to anyone who understood English. In despair, I decided it was vacuous crap, and as I read each page I pencilled a light line through it. I knew I never wanted to read that page again, but without some mark I could not have been sure.

The experience left me with an irrational bias against a discipline whose subject matter is surely as important as anything a discipline could study. It is especially important for psychologists, whose own intellectual traditions too easily tempt them to focus on individuals as if they existed in a social vacuum. It should be doubly important for a psychologist interested in speech and language, which are nothing if not social. But experience can warp as well as expand the mind. It has taken me years to admit that my denunciation was hasty and ill-advised. I take what comfort I can in the belief that academic sociology in 1940 really was almost as windy as I judged it then to be, but I cannot help but wonder what I might have made of it if someone had placed the books of Weber, Durkheim, Mead, Sorel, and Pareto in my hands.

Enough excuses. The deplorable fact is that I am a sociological illiterate. If I were not, if I were accustomed to thinking in terms of social interaction and group dynamics, I would have organized the kiddie lab very differently.

I spent much of World War II trying to improve military voice communications in high noise-level situations. Along with other psychologists, acousticians, and engineers, I was a member of a research team organized by S. S. Stevens— "Smitty" to all who knew him—and called the Harvard Psycho-Acoustic Laboratory. In order to test proposed equipment, or to study the parameters of speech and noise that affect intelligibility, we had one person speak a preselected message into the microphone, then mixed his voice signal with measured amounts of noise, and a crew of listeners wrote down what they thought he had said. What they wrote was scored against what was said; the averaged scores were taken as an estimate of the quality of the communication system.

It was a good introduction to experimental science, and many of my ideas about how research should be administered were cast in that mold. Assemble a team of bright, ambitious young people dedicated to a common problem; give them a facility in which to work and resources on which to draw; make them talk to each other about what they are doing; then sit back and wait for discoveries to pour in. That was essentially the plan J. C. R. Licklider and I followed with considerable success when we organized a group of experimental psychologists to work on human aspects of distant early warning systems at the M.I.T. Lincoln Laboratory in the early 1950s. And some such vision guided me in organizing the Rockefeller University Child Language Facility, affectionately known to those who used it as the kiddie lab.

The academic year 1972–73 was devoted to planning. In the fall of 1972, when I returned to Rockefeller full of the urge to test our new theoretical ideas on children, I sought out Michael Cole. Mike is an experimental psychologist who has outgrown any conception of the laboratory as a cloister and has begun to apply his experimental techniques to children in their natural habitats. The context in which a psychological task is presented to a child can make all the difference in how the child responds; in order to vary the context Mike has not only invaded homes, schools, supermarkets, and day-care centers, but has set up research stations in such different locations as Liberia, Yucatan, and Harlem. Although formal linguistics is not one of his central concerns, his field work requires a sensitivity to languages and he has a long-standing interest in how schooling in general, and reading in particular, can affect the way children think. Even if he had not been my only colleague at Rockefeller actively interested in children, I would still have wanted his advice on how to set up my new program of research.

Mike is a restless spirit. When presented with a problem, he either wants to do something about it or forget it. Usually he does something. When I expressed a desire to rise from my theoretical armchair and embrace psychological reality once again, he was a fountain of support, ideas, action. Yes, I could attend his seminar and learn what he had been doing. But if I wanted to study child language longitudinally, I had to get access to some children. And if I wanted to study their vocabulary, I needed to record their speech and, of course, the context in which it occurred. We had some undeveloped space. Maybe we could get a grant to build a playroom there. Then we could put in television cameras to record what the children said and did. Or I could take recording equipment off campus and study children in more natural settings. I could transcribe what they said, maybe put it into a computer in order to search rapidly for particular things I was interested in. I could also test the children individually, once I knew what particular vocabulary I wanted to follow. He saw uses for television equipment in his own work. We should go together and write a grant proposal.

Which we did. In retrospect, I realize that I absorbed all this into a framework inherited from the Psycho-Acoustic Laboratory (PAL), modified only slightly by my experiences with Licklider at the Lincoln Laboratory and with Bruner at the Center for Cognitive Studies. One of my vivid memories of PAL is how the test crew paced the collection of data. Once a crew had been hired, they appeared at a fixed time for a fixed period every working day. It was unthinkable that they should sit idle in the test room; the only way to prevent it was to design experiments using them. Those who shared the burden not only got the most work done, but were recognized as the really active and productive members. The regular arrival and departure of the test crew set the pulse of the laboratory. I thought that a group of children arriving in the kiddie lab three mornings a week would provide a similar stimulant to the enterprise that Mike and I were discussing.

I am still not entirely clear why a play group did not have the same effect on my laboratory as the test crew had on PAL. In one sense, it did have the desired effect—it paced the collection of video tape recordings of children's behavior in the playroom. But in the sense that was most important to me—the design and execution of experiments—it did not. If I were less naive about social dynamics, I could probably explain it in terms of general and obvious principles applied to the different social circumstances of the two laboratories. But if I were less naive about social dynamics, I would never have expected a similar effect in the first place. The differences, after all, were rather obvious.

For one thing, we were not fighting a war. Each generation is conditioned by its own experiences; those who grew up while the United States was trying to exterminate the Vietnamese will never understand the moral force that united the country in World War II. My generation saw the war against Hitler as a war of good against evil; any able-bodied young man could stomach the shame of civilian clothes only from an inner conviction that what he was doing instead would contribute even more to ultimate victory. We felt no qualms about the fact that we were helping to kill people. The problem was clear: wars are noisy; armies must communicate. By driving ourselves in a race against German and Japanese scientists we shared in an almost religious reflex for national survival. The military were not moral degenerates out of control; they were for, by, and of the people. We had to give them the best equipment in the world. Not too long ago I tried to explain all this to some students. They listened respectfully, they understood the words, they may even have believed that I believed what I was saying. But they could not feel it.

In the kiddie lab none of us felt any compulsion to conduct experiments in order to forestall a national disaster. The children came and left in peace and satisfaction; if we realized that they were rapidly growing through the age we wanted to study, we knew there would always be other children who could take their places. We loved them and they seemed to like us, but our motives for the work were personal—curiosity, ambition, pay. These are powerful motives, but in peacetime they can be satisfied in many ways.

Another difference was that I am not S. S. Stevens. Stevens was a Mormon patriarch who treated the staff as his extended family. He spent sixteen hours a day in the laboratory he built (much of it with his own hands) and was passionately interested in every detail of the work that went on there. He expected a dedication equal to his own from all of us and was never slow to anger when he did not get it. He was, in fact, a demanding tyrant who drove us to do better than we knew. I, on the other hand, am constitutionally incapable of demanding that anybody do anything. I may suggest something, even politely request it, or, in dire straits, confess that I am worried about it; when pushed beyond endurance I may unexpectedly explode, confusing everyone. But basically I see my role as providing an opportunity that younger people can exploit. If they bring me their problems, I share whatever wisdom I can muster, but they are broadly free to follow whatever line (and make whatever mistakes) they choose. This lack of leadership creates as many problems in my laboratory as Stevens's surfeit created in his, but they are very different problems. In particular, if someone does not choose to conduct experiments, I have no way and no will to make him. Moreover, I did not live in the kiddie lab (I commuted between New York and Princeton) and I was not passionately interested in everyting that went on there (my overarching preoccupation was to finish *Language and Perception* with Johnson-Laird). Occasionally I would feel remiss, reorganize the work, set goals, ask for progress reports, stir up trouble, and then retire again to other concerns. Stevens had shown me how to be a driver, but that did not make me one.

The lab might not have needed a strong leader if it had been clearer what we were going to do. At PAL during the war we had tangible products that we were responsible for, and even when there was no particular piece of communication equipment to be improved or evaluated, we were expected to produce technical reports relevant to our mission. In the beginning, the kiddie lab had no comparable mission; our first job was to discover what our second job was going to be. This situation was more of a handicap than any of us realized at the time. It is one thing to join an ongoing research team and find a role to play within its relatively well-defined organization. It is quite a different thing to join a group that is still trying to define itself. We shared an interest in children and in language development, but almost everything else was open for negotiation. An unstructured situation is probably more exciting to the imagination, but the price is a longer lag in producing anything of scientific value. For young people just starting their research careers, that can be a high price.

Still another difference was size. During the war PAL grew to about fifty people. Money was no problem; the military was eager to trade money for time. Experience at the Lincoln Laboratory and at the Center for Cognitive Studies had persuaded me that the minimal size for a productive research group in my field is about ten active workers.

Money was more of a problem at the Center than at PAL or the Lincoln Lab, but during the 1960s it was still possible to keep a group of that size funded. The kiddie lab, on the other hand, was far below critical size and funding was a constant headache.

This is a good place to mention my colleagues.* Robert Jarvella and Keith Stenning were members of my laboratory interested in psychological aspects of language, but neither was particularly interested in the work of the kiddie lab. At this point in time I cannot recall whether I expected them to participate or not. Hoped, maybe, but not expected. In any case, they did their own work and we used them as consultants (and once or twice as psychotherapists) rather than collaborators.

The team actively responsible for the child research deserves a fuller introduction. The key person was Elsa Jaffe Bartlett. In the fall of 1972, shortly after Mike Cole and I had decided to collaborate in setting up a laboratory to study child language, Mike asked Elsa, who was then a student in the Harvard Graduate School of Education, if she would be willing to work on the project. Since Elsa was Courtney Cazden's student, and Courtney had been Roger Brown's student, she provided a comforting tie to my past at Harvard, and I accepted Mike's and Courtney's suggestion that she would be just the person to get our kiddie lab organized. Until we had something for her to organize, however, she worked with Mike in a Harlem Head Start Program. Mike and I were hoping that the research in the kiddie lab and the research in Harlem would run in parallel and mutually-supporting channels, so this use of Elsa's talents during the interval seemed a sensible step toward the realization of that hope. She began working for us full time in the fall of 1973, and assumed the major responsibility for setting up the playroom and getting some children into it. Without Elsa, nothing would have happened.

One of Elsa's most important contributions was Madeleine Dobriner, a nursery school teacher willing to accept

---

*More detailed acknowledgments of the contributions of those who participated in the work are summarized in the Appendix.

responsibility for day-to-day interaction with the children. I had had some vague idea that the research staff would do that, just as we used to share responsibility for the test crew at PAL. A brief episode under that plan quickly brought me to my senses. Even if we had had enough research workers to fill the children's schedule, such an unpredictable regimen would have disturbed both the children and their parents. Madeleine, on the other hand, knew exactly what had to be done.

Elsa and Madeleine together recruited the children and equipped the playroom, Madeleine's supervision delighted both the children and their parents, and Elsa developed unsuspected skills in operating television equipment. I popped in and out, beamed approval and support, and promised them and myself that in just another month or two I would be finished with The Book and able to play a more active part. In the meanwhile, I was relieved that things were getting started with a minimum commitment of my own time and thought.

But where were all the research workers to exploit the fine facility? Cole, Jarvella, and Stenning had their work to pursue and I could hardly fault them for that, for so did I. Although offices were available, we had no budget for more staff. In anticipation of this dilemma, and inspired by what seemed at the time a shrewd plot to have my cake and eat it too, I had arranged to make adjunct appointments. New York has many colleges and universities; their faculties include many gifted people without access to good research facilities. I could offer them a deal. With an adjunct appointment in my laboratory they could earn their salaries for teaching elsewhere and do their research with me. I thought it was an ideal way to assemble a research team at minimal expense.

Since the kiddie lab was designed for closed-circuit television recording, it was natural to look for people with experience both in television and child language. I found two who fitted that description perfectly and both accepted my deal. Joyce Weil, a developmental psychologist, had just resigned from the Children's Television Workshop ("Sesame Street," "The Electric Company," and all that) to take a teaching job at Yeshiva University. John Dore's Ph.D. thesis in linguistics at the City University was based on a detailed analysis of television recordings of how eighteen-month-old children use language in social interaction with their parents.

At this point I was quite optimistic. Not only had I persuaded some talented people to share my adventure, but I had assembled a wide range of skills and knowledge to supplement my own: Elsa was an educational psychologist, Madeleine an early-childhood teacher, Joyce a developmental psychologist, John a linguist, and all this was backstopped in developmental psychology by Mike and in the psychology of language by Keith, Bob, and myself. It turned out to be a paper miracle. In my ignorance of social dynamics, I had overlooked the fact that people trained in different disciplines find it difficult to talk to one another. If I had taken a stronger hand in drawing them all together around the joint enterprise I had envisioned, it might have worked, but just at the time when such leadership was most needed I was still sitting at my typewriter, confident that everything was going well without me.

My sense of well-being was heightened by the fact that David McNeill became interested in the project. During 1973–75 McNeill was at the Institute for Advanced Study, on leave from the University of Chicago. I had maintained my connection with the Institute, thanks to its director, Carl Kaysen, and McNeill and I had offices side by side. He had established a child research facility at Chicago the year before he left, but New York was nearer and more convenient. I welcomed him into the group with undisguised elation.

The roster also included Peter Kranz and Donna Lyons. Peter is a computer expert who had helped me before; when the time came to put our transcriptions into machine-readable form I turned to him again, and he agreed to a part-time arrangement. Donna is my secretary, a job title that does not begin to do her credit, but whatever the title, she was a vital communication link between an often absent head of laboratory and his energetic but uncoordinated colleagues.

We had, in sum, one staff member, one teacher, and two

adjuncts, in addition to myself and some interested helpers. I knew this was too small a group to mount a major attack on the semantic aspects of vocabulary growth, but I believed it would be enough to get started. I wanted the group to grow to five or six staff members and an equal number of assistants and assorted support personnel. Before I could raise money for such a staff, however, I had to have something tangible to sell to potential sources of support. I was optimistic that once the work began it would take on its own shape and direction. I could not predict then exactly how it would grow, but I was boldly confident that when we got into it we would develop exciting and important new ideas, and that money would be no problem. When your head is full of what is going to be, it is sometimes difficult to see clearly what is.

When I think back on it now I can see that I was headed for trouble from the beginning. Maybe Jerry Bruner could have warned me, but in 1972 Jerry moved from Harvard to Oxford, which removed him from my circle of accessible advisors. On the other hand, maybe no one could have warned me. My head was in the clouds. I had this vision of creating a research facility so fine that people would swoon with eagerness to use it, with a flow of new discoveries based on my ideas about the mental lexicon that would dazzle the eyes of funding agencies, who I imagined to have untold resources for child research just waiting to be tapped by a serious scientist like myself. Well, everyone falls on his face occasionally. There is nothing to do but admit it, pick yourself up, and make the best of it.

In this case, making the best of it is not difficult. I am probably too easily disappointed by the inevitable gap between intention and realization. The fact is that some interesting work was done—more than I had any right to expect, given my approach to the whole enterprise. And I did learn a great deal, some of it about children.

A Remarkable Contrast

"What does this show?
What does this show?"
Marvin

Why do psychologists study child language? I have recounted my own reasons—I had some theoretical notions about the dictionary in our heads and I thought I could test them by observing how such a dictionary grows in the heads of children. But that was a personal thing with me. If there were no other reasons to study child language, I could not have persuaded anyone to join me in the enterprise. How did it happen that I could find colleagues already dedicated to such work?

Children's speech, after all, is no great thing. It is often unintelligible; when it is intelligible, it is often ungrammatical. The thoughts expressed are not profound; indeed, they are usually of little consequence outside the immediate context of interaction. Of course, parents find their own child's speech interesting because they find their own child interesting, but surely that is a concern confined to the family situation. Why should serious scientists devote their lives to children's inconsequential vocalizations? What do they hope to learn?

Different individuals have different motives, of course, but there must be some general reasons that all would share, reasons that would be intelligible not only to them, but also to the society at large that supports them in such activities. Probably the most general reason is the one that motivates all science: curiosity about the world and how it works. But that is not enough; not all knowledge is equally valuable. With so many interesting things to be curious about, why child language?

For a psychologist, the value of learning more about the mind and its behavioral manifestations is so fundamental that it is seldom questioned. Given that, the rest follows easily. The developmental approach is a basic strategy in all the biological sciences; language is the most sensitive indicator of mental life. The development of language, therefore, is one of those problems that psychologists simply must study if they are to carry out the proper work of their discipline. Every major psychological theory places great emphasis on the nature of the newborn child and the experiences of the first several years; the development of language is particularly important because it is so clearly tied to the development of mechanisms of thought and self control.

Such is the party line, and I find it very convincing. Personally, however, I think child language would not have attracted quite as much attention as it has if it were not extremely interesting in its own right. Consider what actually happens. A child is born knowing nothing of the language that he or she will eventually learn—or of any other language. An adult in a foreign land at least knows what language is and what has to be learned; there is no way to explain to an infant what language is, or how to use it, or any of its confusing subtleties. The child has to figure it all out from the speech and behavior of others, with no tools of symbolic thought or analysis to help, and little to guide the learning but an instinctive impulse to communicate. It is as if a novice had to learn to play chess by observing the play of others, with no explanation of the rules or general strategies or the object of the game. It is like that, only much worse: the language game is enormously more complicated than chess.

One might feel inclined to say the task was impossible if every normal child did not master it in a few short years. That every child learns to talk is such a commonplace observation that we have to stop and think about it to appreciate what a miracle of development it really is. And once it is appreciated, it is almost impossible to suppress your curiosity. I find it one of the most challenging mysteries on the agenda of psychological science.

So that is one reason psychologists study child language: they hope to discover principles of growth and learning powerful enough to account for this amazing and uniquely human accomplishment.

Psychologists would probably not be allowed the luxury of studying this enigma, however, if their results did not promise benefits of more general value to society. There must be practical reasons as well. One obvious place to look for them is in the field of education.

We invest enormous sums every year in our schools and colleges in the faith that formal education has both personal and social value, and we are repeatedly disappointed by the results. The teachers, who stand at the center of this drama of disappointed faith, recognize clearly that educational failure is all too often linguistic failure. Schooling begins with the teaching of reading and writing; then these linguistic tools are used to unlock all the further stores of accumulated knowledge. A child who fails to master the basic tools will, almost necessarily, be severely handicapped in the competitive environment of the American classroom. There are, therefore, compelling practical reasons behind the educators' appeal for help from those who claim to understand child language.

Now, these two reasons, the scientific and the practical, stand in sharp, almost painful, contrast. On the one hand, we are fascinated that children can learn language so well in the home and, on the other hand, we are frustrated and puzzled that they have so much trouble learning and using further linguistic skills in the schoolroom. One response to this remarkable contrast is to criticize our schools, to claim that they do something to many children that turns off their natural impulse to learn. But, lacking any account of what the schools do or what, if anything, is turned off, such criticism is more demoralizing than constructive.

I believe that students of child language who want to answer the educators' appeal for help can do so most effectively by discovering the conditions that facilitate language learning in the earliest years. Only then, if ever, will we know how to create comparable conditions in our schools. It may turn out, of course, that the spontaneous apprenticeship that works so well at home cannot be simply transferred to the school situation; I would not like to be counted as an uncritical advocate of some new form of progressive education. But perhaps even the failure of direct transfer would not be a serious obstacle if we understood better the general principles that make early learning so effective. In one form or another, a hope that this contrast might be reduced is another reason to study child language.

But enough of reasons. Back to my story.

What's in a Theory?

"What kind of game is it?"
Don

Since it was a theory that started the whole thing, rules for reasonable exposition dictate that I should start my account the same way. Reasonable or not, this poses a problem.

Language and Perception has more than 700 closely argued pages. As we were finishing it, Johnson-Laird and I asked ourselves whether, now that we knew what we wanted to say, we could write the same book in half the length. Like many other long-winded authors before us, we decided we did not have time. Now I would like to reduce the whole thing to ten pages. The problem with reasonable exposition is that I am not able to do it.

The book is about the lexical component of language. In particular, it is about how lexical knowledge might be stored in a person's memory so that he can use it at the rapid rates of conversational speech. The lexicon, as some astute linguist once remarked, is a repository for exceptions. Not only must thousands of words be accounted for, but almost every word has its own idiosyncrasies. One of the firmest conclusions I reached as a consequence of writing the book was that no simple psychological principle could ever account for all of the complicated and heterogeneous information that people learn when they learn the vocabulary of their language. Anyone who thinks he could give an adequate account of it in ten pages is a fool. Maybe those who think they could do it in 700 pages are fools, too.

One way to look at a lexicon is to divide it up into fields of related words. For example, take all the names of animals. There are terms at several levels of generality: *sparrow, bird, animal* or *collie, dog, mammal, animal.* At any given level of generality there are alternatives: *sparrow, robin, canary,* or *collie, terrier, poodle.* All the words in this field can be related to one another; when we trace out the relations, they form a large hierarchy, or taxonomy. Hierarchical organization is common, especially among nouns. Does this imply something about lexical memory? A person who knows the meaning of *dog* knows what dogs are, of course, but he also knows that dogs are animals. Does that mean that when he hears or says *dog* he thinks of animals? Or of *animal?* That is one kind of question the book wrestled with.

When I first got into this kind of research I had some silly notion that all words are related to one another in an enormous hierarchical tree, with *idea* or *entity* as the most general word of all. If I had realized how complicated it really is, I probably would not have gone into it. Now I know (I could have known it at the time, but enthusiasm overpowered scholarship) that different lexical fields can be organized very differently. For example, the best way to organize color terms is in a circle; the best way to organize kin terms is at the corners of a three or four dimensional solid; names for times can be mapped onto a line; verbs of motion seem to require some complex lattice of shared concepts that is difficult to visualize spatially. Trees, circles, corners, lines, lattices, and so on. Does this variety of organizing principles imply something about the human mind? Some concepts are required to organize a lexical field and others provide the core concept to be organized. What is the difference? And what about words with several senses that occur in more than one lexical field? The book wrestled with this kind of question, too.

Words in isolation may signal something, but they do not assert anything. For assertions, we require sentences. Any theory of lexical knowledge that ignores the fact that words and their meanings must be combined in sentences to form the infinite variety of sentential concepts of which the human mind is capable is useless. The book also wrestled with that.

Words—some words, at least—can refer to or identify concrete things. A theory of lexical knowledge that treated only the relations between words and words, or between words and sentences, would also be useless. The relation of words to things had to be wrestled with, too.

All in all, we did a great deal of wrestling, since the way you deal with any one of these problems limits the ways you can deal with the others. "Wrestle" is the correct verb; "solve" would be much too strong. The ideas we brought to bear came from psychology, linguistics, computer science, logic, philosophy; definitive solutions of problems within one of these disciplines are hard to come by, but when you try to gather them together it becomes hopeless. We wrestled, and hoped the result would be a framework for a new branch of cognitive psychology, one we baptised with the ugly name "psycholexicology." The wrestling is as important a part of the book as are the conclusions we eventually endorsed, and nobody is going to reduce *that* to ten pages.

Not all of the issues raised in *Language and Perception* are appropriate for developmental studies. I eventually selected three that my junior faculty seemed to be particularly interested in: color, space, and time. With apologies for all that cannot be said, therefore, I can serve my present purpose and give something of the flavor of the enterprise by reviewing those three very briefly.

Color, space, and time make an interesting triad. Once upon a time some philosophers announced to their readers that, since all knowledge of the world must enter the mind via the doors of the senses, a careful study of perception would reveal to us the structure of human knowledge and the means whereby men acquire it. This careful study was duly undertaken along the best scientific lines available at the time. That is to say, perceptions were analyzed into combinations of sensory elements in much the same way that chemists were then analyzing all forms of matter into combinations of chemical elements. One consequence was that some who followed this approach came to think of the visual world as if it were a mosaic of spots, where each spot could differ from every other spot in terms of its color and location, and all the spots together formed the picture seen in the mind. The arrangement of sensory cells in the retina of the eye seemed to lend plausibility to this idea, as if each receptor cell contributed one spot to the total mosaic. The mosaic of spots would change, however, as the world changed or as the eyes moved, so in addition to color and location, a time dimension had to be added. Thus, the three dimensions of elementary spots were color, location, and time. Our junior faculty's interest in these three was an odd echo from the history of psychological studies of perception—an echo so faint it might not have been heard except by someone deeply engrossed in the relation between perception and language. Theories of perception have long since outgrown any simplistic reduction of the visual world to elementary color-spot-moments, but the need to explain how people perceive and talk about color, space, and time has persisted. And so has the belief that a careful study of such aspects of perception can tell us something fundamental about the human mind and the knowledge structures it builds.

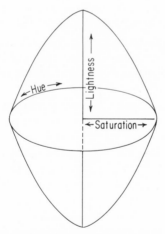

COLOR. Color terms provide an ideal example of a semantic field. A semantic field generally consists of a lexical field and a conceptual field. The lexical field consists of all the words that are used to express a related set of concepts; the conceptual field consists of a set of concepts related in what might be regarded as a layman's implicit equivalent of a scientific theory. A description of a semantic field must provide a description of how the lexical field expresses, or maps onto, the conceptual field.

In English, the lexical field of color terms includes such words as: *color, red, black, fuschia, yellow, puce, pink, green, gamboge, blue, magenta, white, lavender, gray, orange, brown, crimson.* English has thousands of color names, and part of the task of describing this field is to put them into some relation to one another that makes psychological sense. The word *color* is the general superordinate term; all the others are terms for special kinds of colors.

The conceptual field of color is illustrated graphically by the color solid, a representation that evolved as the result of more than a century of research. In general, three dimensions are required to specify a color sensation: hue, saturation, and lightness. The hues are generally arranged in a circle that forms the perimeter of the color solid. The achromatic colors—white, gray, black—form a scale of lightness running through the center of the circle of hues, providing the vertical dimension of the color solid. Saturation gives the location of the color between the center and the perimeter: the most saturated colors are on the perimeter and saturation decreases as the neutral center is approached. Every color sensation can be located somewhere in this three-dimensional solid.

The color solid is not a concrete object available for inspection; it is a conceptual structure, a representation of the theory of color perception. Color terms can be defined by mapping them onto the color solid—by giving their focus and boundaries in the color solid. For example, the focus for the word *red* would be the most typical, highly saturated red on the perimeter of the solid. Of course, other colors adjacent to focal red will also be called *red; red* is defined by a volume in the color solid. But the farther you move away from focal red, the less certain you become that the color really deserves the name *red.* The point at which the majority of judges would stop calling it *red* and start calling it something else—*gray, orange, purple, white, black, brown, pink*—is the boundary of the *red* category. In general, judgments of focal colors are relatively stable and independent of the particular language you happen to speak, but judgments of category boundaries are variable and depend on what other color terms you are allowed to use.

Psychological experiments have shown that any chromatic color can be described by using combinations of only four terms: *red, yellow, green,* and *blue.* These four are the so-called psychological primaries. Orange, for example, can be described as 50% red and 50% yellow. In these experiments, however, no colors could be found that were described as combinations of red and green, or as combinations of blue and yellow. Red/green and yellow/blue are opponent processes; the visual nervous system has evolved in such a way that light will excite either the red or green response, but not both, and either the yellow or blue response, but not both. Conceptually, that fact is represented by placing red opposite to green in the color circle, and yellow opposite to blue. Lexically, it is represented by the absence of any color terms that would be defined as, say, a reddish green, or a bluish yellow.

On the basis of extensive psychological and neurophysiological evidence, therefore, six color terms can be selected as basic: four terms denoting chromatic colors, *red, yellow, green,* and *blue,* and, since black/white are also opponent processes, two terms denoting achromatic colors, *black* and *white.* Since these denote primary colors, it is reasonable to call them the primary color terms. Secondary color terms can be defined in terms of these primary colors: *cyan,* for example, is greenish blue; *puce* is between red and reddish blue, but low in lightness and low to moderate in saturation; and so on. There are thousands of secondary color terms, most of which are seldom used, and they can be supplemented by such phrases as *the color of ashes, like a ripe lemon,* or even *the color of Henry's new shoes.* Thus, we find a hierarchy of color terms: the word *color* is at the top; the six primary terms are at the second level; thousands of secondary terms are at the third level.

For someone interested in the relation between language and perception, color terms provide a good place to work, because so much is known about color, color perception, and color terminologies. Color terms are also relatively difficult for children to learn, which makes them interesting because it violates one's intuition that it should be easy to learn names for such an obvious and important feature of the perceptual world.

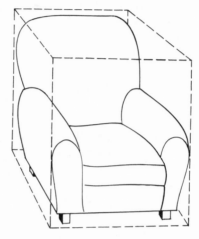

SPACE. Spatial terms, unlike color terms, do not form a simple semantic field. Because space is so important for our daily activities, we have a great variety of ways of talking about it. Perhaps spatial terms could be divided up into many different semantic fields: geographical place names; names of different kinds of shapes, barriers, boundaries, and containers; directional terms like *up* and *down*; relational terms like *in, on,* and *under*; side names like *top* and *bottom, front* and *back*; pointing words like *here* and *there*; size terms like *big* and *little, thick* and *thin*. All of these various groups of words (and more) express different aspects of our general concept of space.

Out of this impressive array of lexical resources for expressing spatial relations I will select only one, the system of labelling intrinsic sides of concrete objects. The lexical field includes the words *top, bottom, front, back, right,* and *left*, with *side* as the superordinate term. The conceptual field is the representation of any concrete, physical object as three-dimensional, with six orthogonal sides (regardless of its actual shape).

These words can be used in two different ways. When

they are used deictically (*deiktos* is a Greek word meaning "show" or "point to"), they refer to a side of the object that must be determined relative to the viewer. When they are used intrinsically, they refer to a side of the object that is independent of the viewer. The difference is illustrated most easily with *right* and *left*. Imagine that you are facing John and Mary, who are located side by side in such a way that John is opposite your left hand and Mary is opposite your right hand. As you view them, you can say "John is to the left of Mary," meaning *left* from your point of view; that is the deictic use, since it would change if you walked around behind them. But note that (if they are facing you) this situation puts John next to Mary's right hand, so you can also say "John is to Mary's right," where *right* is independent of your point of view; that is the intrinsic use, since it depends on the fact that Mary has an intrinsic right and left side that stay the same regardless of your point of view or her orientation. That the same situation can be described using either *right* or *left* should cause considerable ambiguity and confusion, but in fact people seldom become confused unless they stop and try to describe what they are doing.

The first semantic feature, therefore, is the distinction between deictic and intrinsic sides. The second feature involves the number of intrinsic sides that an object has. Objects like rocks and balls have no intrinsic sides: whatever part is uppermost is its *top*, whatever part is facing you is its *front*, and whatever part is to your right is its *right*. For objects with no intrinsic sides, these words can only be used deictically. However, many objects like tables and drinking glasses have an intrinsic *top* and *bottom*, but no other intrinsic sides; if you turn them over, the (intrinsic) top is on the (deictic) bottom, but their *front/back* and *left/right* depend on your point of view. Objects like chairs and bookcases that have intrinsic tops can also have an intrinsic *front* and *back*; if you turn them around, the (intrinsic) front is in the (deictic) back. Moreover, if an object has both an intrinsic top and an intrinsic front, then it will also have an intrinsic *right* and *left*, but which is which depends on a third semantic feature. If the object is one that you charactertistically face, like bookcases or newspapers, then its right side is the one opposite your right hand as you face it; if the object is one that you are characteristically inside of, like chairs or clothing, then its intrinsic right side is the one opposite your left hand as you face it (the one nearest your right hand when you are inside it). Living organisms (and their replicas) are a special case—we characteristically face them, but we label their sides as if we were inside them.

That is the general system. It requires considerable learning of which objects have what intrinsic sides and which objects are characteristically faced or entered. Not all adults master it completely—the *left/right* convention seems to cause the most trouble—and even those who do master it would have considerable difficulty explaining what they had learned. Because there is a lot to learn, and because children must pick it up from adults who are unable to explain it, we thought that the system of labelling intrinsic sides would be a good one to look for in our young charges.

Before Now   **Now**   **After Now**
(past)   **(future)**

TIME. Like spatial terms, temporal terms do not constitute a simple semantic field. Here we can distinguish such lexical varieties as: the metric system of dates, hours, minutes; relational terms like *before* and *after*, *until* and *since*; adverbs like *eventually, subsequently, often*; deictic terms like *now, yesterday*; verbs like *begin, recur, postpone*. The expression of temporal relations is further complicated by the tense system, which adds a grammatical dimension to the lexical resources of English. Time is so important in our culture that we have evolved a great variety of ways to express it.

The conceptual field in this case is relatively simple, at least by comparison with the complexity of its lexical field and grammatical conventions. The graphical representation of the time concept is a straight line extending from the past (usually on the left) through the present into the future (usually on the right). It is a tribute to the inventiveness of the human mind that so many linguistic complexities can be hung from something as humble as the time line. On the other hand, the time line is much like the number line (onto which it is frequently mapped), and everyone knows the complexities that mathematicians have found in the number line.

The time line represents a linear ordering of moments, so the ordering relation expressed by *before* is fundamental. *Before* is one of several words that express both temporal and spatial relations: in "He stood before the king," for example, *before* is ambiguous between *in front of* and *at an earlier time than*. It is only its temporal sense, that event A occurred at an earlier time than event B, that concerns us here. For momentary events, *after* is the converse of *before*. That is to say, if A and B are two momentary events, then to say that A is before B is logically equivalent to saying that B is after A.

This logical equivalence is not a psychological equivalence, however. Consider the following four ways to say the same thing:

(1)   A is before B.
(2)   B is after A.
(3)   Before B, A.
(4)   After A, B.

People do not find these equally easy to understand: (1) is the easiest and (2) is the hardest. The reasons for these differences have been debated by several psychologists interested in how people understand time language. One factor seems to be the order in which the events are mentioned in the sentence: (1) and (4) mention them in the order in which they occur—they are forward sentences; (2) and (3) mention them in the reverse order—they are backward sentences. Another factor seems to be a tendency to think that the event described in the main clause comes first: (1) and (3) describe the first event in the main clause; (2) and (4) describe the first event in the subordinate clause. These two factors alone would suffice to explain why (1) is easiest (it is forward, with the first event in the main clause) and (2) is hardest (it is backward, with the first event in the subordinate clause). But other factors may be at work as well.

Although the temporal relation expressed by *before* or *after* is fundamental to the concept of the time line, *before* and *after* are only two of several words in this lexical subfield. We can also use *and then, next, when, while, but first, until, since,* and so on. The logical entailments of these terms are analyzed in *Language and Perception,* but the details need not detain us here.

If event A is at some time before event B, then it is always before event B. On the other hand, if event A is before *now,* then at some past time it was after *now;* it was once in the future (after *now*), then momentarily in the present (right *now*), and subsequently in the past (before *now*). Thus, *now* is a deictic term—its meaning (the time it refers to, or identifies) depends on when it is used; in order to understand what a speaker meant when he said *now,* we must know when he was speaking.

Now is the anchor of the English tense system, which assumes that *now* is the moment of speech. As a first approximation, we can say that the past tense signals that the event referred to occurred before the moment of speaking, before *now;* the future tense signals that it will occur after the moment of speaking, after *now.* If we simplify by considering only the concept of *pastness* (which is the tense system's equivalent of *before*) and by ignoring the progressive forms, we find one way to express *presentness* and three ways to express *pastness* in the indicative mood:

(1) Present   We walk
(2) Past   We walked
(3) Present perfect   We have walked
(4) Past perfect   We had walked

The availability of different ways to express pastness shows that the system is more complicated than our first approximation would suggest. If all we wanted to say was that e, the time of the event, was before s, the time of speech, we would need only one way to express it. But the system provides three ways.

The nature of the complication can be seen most clearly in

(4), the past perfect. It seems incomplete to say "We had walked"; we feel that there must have been another event between the time of walking, e, and the time at which the sentence is uttered, s: "We had walked until we bought a car," for example. In this expanded form we see that there are really three things being ordered in time: first, walking; then, buying; finally, speaking. Let us call the time of this intermediate event r, the time of reference. The past perfect says, in effect, "I am referring to a time r in the past (before s), and the event I am describing occurred at a time e before r." In brief, e before r before s. The past perfect expresses what some linguists have called the-past-in-the-past.

Once we recognize that these sentences order three times, not just two, it is a simple matter to extend the analysis to the other three tenses:

(1) Present   We walk $e = r = s$
(2) Past   We walked $e = r$ before s
(3) Present perfect   We have walked e before $r = s$
(4) Past perfect   We had walked e before r before s

The rules are that "past" means "r before s" and that "perfect" means "e before r." Even though the concept of time is relatively simple, it is clear that children have a lot to learn before they master the linguistic intricacies of the ways we use this concept.

Although these accounts of the language of color, space, and time are dangerously oversimplified, I think enough is left to suggest the kinds of analyses that Phil Johnson-Laird and I reported in the book. They should also suggest that a three-year-old who tries to master these systems undertakes an important learning task—one well worth serious study.

A feature of this learning that I find particularly challenging is its implicit nature. No one would suggest that children are learning to state the rules explicitly in the way I have just tried to do; few adults are able to do that. But they are learning to conform to those rules. How children can learn to conform to rules that they will never learn to state poses a deep question for students of development in general, and for students of language development in particular.

The Kiddie Lab

"Want to play together,
you and me, Kevin?"
Don

Since the central function for which the kiddie lab was designed was television, perhaps I should present it as a dramatic script: cast, setting, lines, action. I will get around to all that, but in my own way. I want to describe the stage setting for our video dramas, but first, in keeping with my goal of illustrating how things come to pass in the world of research, I need to explain how we got money and permission to build it.

The kiddie lab was more than a stage setting. It was a laboratory in a laboratory. At most universities it would have been a laboratory in a department, but Rockefeller is not like most universities. For many years it was the Rockefeller Institute for Medical Research; as a research institute it was organized into laboratories and the work was directed by heads of laboratories. That structure persisted after Detlev Bronk changed the name to The Rockefeller University in 1965. According to the catalogue, "Laboratories, rather than conventional categorical departments, are the fundamental units of the University." My lab is called Experimental Psychology, not because I cover all of that large field but because I have refused any professional designation other than experimental psychologist. William K. Estes's is called Mathematical Psychology and Michael Cole's is Comparative Human Cognition. It is a little odd that such an institution should be called a university at all, since it is limited to the sciences and has no undergraduate body. But whatever is is called, it is shaped for the support and implementation of research. Head of Laboratory at Rockefeller is a shrewdly optimized position from which to work as a practicing scientist. Of course, you have to go to outside sources to raise most of your own money to support your research, but that is true at all American universities.

Since most psychological research on human subjects is conducted with undergraduates, the absence of a student body is something of an inconvenience. On the other hand, if one suspects that college sophomores may not be representative of the population at large, the inconvenience can be viewed as an advantage. Since you must go off-campus to recruit experimental subjects in any case, you may as well recruit whomever best suits your needs. Thus, working with children poses only a few more problems than would any other kind of human experimental psychology.

In 1968 and 1969 the University was planning for the use of a new building then under construction. Bill Estes and I requested that our laboratories be together, the University consented, and we were given the fourth floor of the Tower Building to divide. Each floor has four equal-sized bays; Bill drew up plans for two of them and I drew up plans for the other two. When I went on leave in 1970, however, plans for my half of the floor were abandoned. When I returned in the fall of 1972, the University generously undertook to outfit one of the remaining two areas for my use, and agreed to hold the other uncommitted until my research program required it.

At that time I was thinking of getting into child language more slowly. I was going to finish the book in 1972–73, spend full time in 1973–74 studying developmental psychology and trying a few pilot experiments, and maybe in 1974–75 start to grow into a larger enterprise with a larger staff, laboratory, and budget. If I had followed that schedule, I would have been better prepared for what was to transpire, but events moved faster than I anticipated.

Once Mike Cole and I had decided we needed a place to study children intensively over a period of several months, we took our plans to Carl Pfaffmann who, as vice-president of the University, had general responsibility for the program in the behavioral sciences. He approved of our idea and began at once, with his usual effectiveness, to search for sources of support. He discovered that The Grant Foundation might be interested in receiving a proposal for such a research facility at Rockefeller, the Engineering Department quickly drew up plans and estimated costs, and by March 1, 1973, we had received a grant of $150,000 to build The Rockefeller University Child Language Facility in the empty space on the fourth floor of the Tower Building.

Our dream came true a year ahead of my schedule. It is stupid to quarrel with success, but I knew I was not ready for it. Mike told me not to worry; he might as well have told a pig not to grunt. I threw myself simultaneously into planning the facility, studying developmental psychology, trying to finish The Book, and worrying about how it would all come out. Construction of my first area was completed in April 1973 and I moved into it as work began on the second, which was completed that summer.

The Grant Foundation grant provided about $100,000 for construction and furnishings, and $50,000 for equipment; the equipment money was split between a closed circuit television system ($35,000) and a minicomputer ($15,000). It turned out that we had overestimated construction costs and underestimated the cost of furnishings and special equipment, but The Grant Foundation was wonderfully accommodating in allowing us to shift funds from one account to the other. And when some of the work fell behind schedule, they extended the term of the grant to let us finish.

As soon as the money was available we began spending it. A computer was ordered with the advice of Bob Schoenfeld, our local expert on such matters; it arrived on schedule (almost) and Peter Kranz set to work writing programs for it. We asked for bids on the video system and settled on the Windsor Electronic Company as the contractor. The Office of Buildings and Grounds supervised the construction work. Everything seemed to be shaping up for a completed facility by fall, and Elsa Bartlett was given the go-ahead to furnish the playroom and assemble a suitable group of children to appear in October.

The central feature of the facility was the playroom, 22

feet square, which provided the stage setting for our little dramas. Thanks to Elsa, the room was equipped for a variety of activities: blocks, toys, housekeeping, story-telling, and so on, each in a particular area. (Across the hall was a special bathroom equipped with a toilet and washbasin of dimensions appropriate to three-year-old children.) Television cameras on the ceiling in each corner provided complete coverage of the playroom. The video equipment was controlled from an adjacent room, and a large one-way mirror made it possible to watch the group directly from the darkened control room. Almost no one used the mirror; it was easier to watch the four television screens, one for each camera.

The four cameras could be operated remotely from the control console by means of switches for "pan," "tilt," and "zoom." Most of the operator's burden was aiming the cameras, especially when trying to follow a child taking a rapid diagonal or irregular path across the room—but after a little practice we could usually hit the right switches in the right directions at the right time. The operator also had to choose which one of the four video signals would be recorded on magnetic tape for subsequent analysis, but that was a simple task once we learned to visualize which corner of the room each set of controls was connected to. Understandably, the quality of our recordings improved progressively through the year. One important lesson we learned was to fiddle with the controls as little as possible.

The stern maxim that children should be seen and not heard was not for us. We were primarily concerned with recording what the children were saying, and we took particular pains in designing the audio system. We put a rug on the floor and acoustical tile on the ceiling in order to quiet the room and reduce echoes. I was told that the rug disqualified us for official certification as a day care center, which meant we had to keep our group below the legal limit in size. This limitation was no inconvenience, however, because the children often talked at the same time— the more children there were, the more they overlapped and the harder transcription became. I felt that our group was too large for good recording, but Elsa and Madeleine Dobriner argued that a smaller group would not be sufficiently spontaneous and natural. Since one or two of the children were usually absent, I did not press my point, but I am still convinced that I was right. I know a lot more about acoustics than about children.

A single microphone hanging from the center of the ceiling recorded the teacher's voice fairly well, but not the children's. In order to obtain a distinct speech signal from each child, regardless of location, they all wore cordless microphones: a microphone plus a miniature radio transmitter and broadcast antenna, powered by small batteries. In order to hang this gear (14 ounces) on our little people, smocks were obtained and pockets sewn on the backs to hold the transmitters. The microphone was sewn into the front pocket, and each child trailed a thin gray wire that looked like a tail and served as an antenna. In the control console there was a separate receiver tuned to each child's transmitter; the operator could adjust the signal level from each receiver before mixing them and recording them together on the video-tape. Peter Kranz had pointed out to me that an eight-channel recorder would have given us separate and clearer signals from each child, but we had not allowed for that in our budget and had to make do with the mixed signal. It was an expensive economy.

The cordless microphones were a good idea, but in the long run they caused us far more grief than the video equipment. The model we had was temperamental. I could imagine keeping one of them operating fairly reliably, but six or eight at once was enough to insure that at least one would be acting up at any given time. "Acting up" consisted of fading at particular locations in the room, aging batteries, picking up other radio transmissions in the area, static, and other mysterious changes of state that, for all I know, may have been correlated with phases of the moon or train schedules in New Zealand. Throughout this period the newspapers were full of stories about electronic "bugging" and the marvelous miniature equipment available for unobtrusive eavesdropping, but when I asked our contractor to replicate these technological miracles in the kiddie lab he replied that he had already given us the best equipment on the market. That was only one of the sources of tension that developed between the contractor and us.

I have described the video and audio systems as they were originally planned, and as they eventually came to function when they were finally installed. In the interim, things did not materialize in quite the manner I had been led to expect. To recount our various confrontations with the contractor who had agreed to install and maintain the video and audio systems by September would do credit neither to him nor to me, so I will pass over it quickly with the observation that the equipment was not installed until after Christmas and was not working properly until March. At this distance in time I can try to view it philosophically as just another illustration of the difficulties involved in conducting scientific research. Elsa, however, who had to make what tapes she could in October and November hunched in a corner of the playroom with a handheld camera, formed a stronger opinion that I doubt time will ever dim.

In addition to the playroom there was also the red rug room. At the time I was designing the first installment of my laboratory—back when I planned a leisurely year or two to tool up for the kiddie lab—I set aside one small room for experiments with children. Tom Bever had impressed on me that, if children are to be comfortable and behave normally, such a room should look as much like a room in a private home as possible. So I requested wall-to-wall carpeting in a happy color, which proved to be bright red. Being a special room, it deserved a special name, but no one proposed anything appropriate and eventually it became known simply as the red rug room. It turned out to be very useful for individual, one-to-one testing of the children. In the playroom it was often difficult to decide whether a child knew something or was imitating other children; in the red rug room there were no other children to imitate. It also turned out to be a convenient place to transcribe the tapes, but I will save that part of the story until later.

These two rooms, the playroom and the red rug room, symbolized for me the two styles of research I hoped would flourish equally in the kiddie lab: naturalistic and experimental. In the playroom we would collect samples of the spontaneous language and behavior of children in a natural setting. In the red rug room we would conduct experiments to test particular hypotheses derived from the naturalistic observations. Many laboratories at Rockefeller rely on the Animal House to provide animals needed in experiments. My biomedical colleagues may have thought of our arrangement in an analogous way, as if we were keeping our experimental animals in the playroom and taking them into the red rug room as needed for experiments. To speak of the playroom as our metaphorical animal house, however, would have provoked unanswerable objections from our loyal band of parents; fortunately, the parallel was never made explicit. The naturalistic-experimental contrast, on the other hand, was an explicit part of my thinking and talking about the kiddie lab, and, to me, the experimental research was the more important of the two. After all, my lab *is* called Experimental Psychology.

What happened, of course, was that the regular arrival and departure of the play group did pace the collection of naturalistic recordings, but the experimental component fell behind. The red rug room was empty most of the time. Elsa Bartlett could not use it; during the time the children were available, Elsa was running the video equipment. John Dore did not use it; John's concern was with the naturalistic use of language in the playroom. Joyce Weil might have used it, but she was heavily committed to developing the courses she was teaching for the first time at Yeshiva University; Joyce made some use of it during this first year and probably would have made more if the budget had permitted hiring research assistants. Mark Altom, a student in Bill Estes's lab, tried to use it for studies of color discrimination, but Elsa (unknown to me) ordered him to stop. Mike Cole did not use it; he was busy conducting experiments elsewhere. And I did not use it; I reproach myself more for not setting a good example of red rug room research than for any other of my failings in this enterprise.

From October through December 1973 the playroom operated, but the kiddie lab did not; between January and April 1974 the kiddie lab was up and running, at least on one leg. Thus it eased gradually into existence over a period of months while I grew accustomed to knowing it was there, but had an excuse for not initiating any research. Perhaps that attitude persisted even after the excuse had vanished. In any case, I settled for working indirectly—by advising Elsa Bartlett and Joyce Weil and discussing the problems of accurate transcriptions with John Dore and Peter Kranz—and the collection of naturalistic recordings dominated the execution of formal experiments.

In the absence of adequate resources to mount a program of formal experimentation, Elsa made a valiant effort to conduct exploratory experiments in the playroom. She formulated various questions about colors and spatial relations that Madeleine could ask the children—usually by taking one child aside while the others continued their play—and began developing some of the ideas that eventually did lead to formal experiments. What those preliminary interviews lacked in the way of experimental controls they more than made up for in convenience—a question could be asked one day and revised or improved the next. Joyce also used the playroom for experiments cleverly designed to test the children's understanding of *before* and *after*—by asking them to execute or relay commands incorporating those words.

In retrospect, I realize that those initial explorations were indispensible for the subsequent development of more formal, better controlled, publishable experiments. I have wondered subsequently why they seemed so unsatisfactory to me at the time. In part, I was still under the sway of my experience at the Psycho-Acoustic Laboratory, where our mission was well-defined and adequate techniques for formal experimentation had already been developed. In part, too, I was still under the sway of my former collaborations; I had expected to share the use of the kiddie lab with Mike Cole, to follow his lead in exploiting the video recordings. But Mike had as many other things to do as I did. I thought that Mike wanted the recordings as much as I did, and therefore felt committed to continuing them—and frustrated that their continuation seemed to place demands on our resources that left nothing over for experiments of the kind I imagined. But try as I may to place the blame on someone else, I keep coming back to the fact that I was not thinking clearly about the problems of the kiddie lab. I had a general notion of what I wanted it to become, but no clear plan for growing into it.

My notion was to use the red rug room to test hypotheses derived from naturalistic observations in the playroom. It should have required no great insight on my part to realize that such a notion implied that we would first make some naturalistic observations, then develop some hypotheses, and only after that would we be in a position to conduct some experimental tests of those hypotheses. Maybe I did realize it. I do not remember clearly whether I did or not, but if I did, it would help to explain why I was at first so complacent about the naturalistic component outrunning the experimental. It would have been impossible for both types of research to start up at the same pace, even if there had been enough people available to do both kinds of work.

Planning an experiment takes time—time to develop test materials, settle on methods for presenting them and recording responses, time to try out the materials and methods in advance to be sure they work—and before you can begin planning you have to know what the experiment is going to be about. In the fall of 1973 I was not even clear which of the various lexical fields that Phil Johnson-Laird and I had tried to analyze were appropriate for longitudinal tracking with three-year-olds. I suspected that color names might be appropriate and Elsa had done her doctoral research on spatial language of children around this age, so those two were plausible candidates. Time language, which Joyce Weil had studied, struck me (incorrectly) as too abstract for this age. But there were many other conceptual domains that I would have liked to study. It was only after the junior faculty had spoken that these three—color, space, and time—stood out as the best intersection of our theories and the children's competence.

The next step was to try to elicit discussion of these topics from the children in the playroom. Madeleine was a valuable source of advice and ideas; her control of the group was so firm that she could conduct short, one-to-one interviews in a corner of the playroom in order to give Elsa a better line on what was possible. In one way or another, Elsa and Madeleine did a lot of what is usually called pilot testing, but none of it shaped up into anything that I could recognize as an experiment. It is particularly difficult to incorporate an experiment into a naturalistic setting without disrupting it, making it unnatural. You must know a great deal about the structure and function of the phenomenon you want to experiment on—exactly the kind of knowledge we lacked in the beginning.

I began to think more and more of the first group of children as a pilot group who would help us develop our hypotheses and an appropriate battery of lexical tests that we could use on subsequent groups or that we could take off-campus for cross-sectional studies. I gradually grasped what had to be done and even saw, with some unjustifiable resentment, that I should provide leadership in doing it. But I never dropped all my other commitments and devoted full time to organizing the experimental program that I wanted. If someone had confronted me with my derelictions, I might have been shamed into action, but no one seemed surprised that the Professor and Head of Laboratory had other things to do.

One of the other things I had to do was visit China. In the summer of 1973, while the playroom was under construction, I took a month away to participate in a summer work group on reading that was organized by the National Institute of Education. I know very little about the teaching of reading, but I have been a loud and persistent advocate of its educational importance; that was my only qualification to serve as chairman of a group who really did know something about reading. In any case, they produced a fine report that I, as chairman, spent September and October editing. Since it became known in some circles as the Miller Report, I achieved the status of reading expert overnight.

Once you are an expert, anything can happen. William Kessen, who had been a member of the reading group, was shortly thereafter asked to serve as chairman of an exchange delegation to visit the People's Republic of China and observe their methods of child care and rearing. Kessen included me in the delegation and assigned me the task of finding out how they teach reading and writing in Chinese schools. Since I knew no Chinese, my qualifications as an expert on reading Chinese were even slimmer than on reading English, but I was not going to let an excess of modesty deprive me of this opportunity. November 1973 was therefore spent about as far from the kiddie lab as our planet allows. When I got back, early in December, the video and audio systems were still not working.

As I recall it now, however, the main reason for my sluggish response was The Book. Phil and I kept up a running discussion of whether we should do it right or do it Thursday; doing it right always got the higher priority. But transatlantic collaboration is difficult and new ideas could be hashed out thoroughly only during his periodic visits, and so the writing went slowly. We both realized that the manuscript had developed a will of its own. We were its loyal servants, not its imperious masters. Until its demands were fulfilled, neither of us was a free agent. The kiddie lab actually aggravated the problem of the book—I had to include all I was learning about child language, which gave it a stronger developmental emphasis than we had initially intended. It dragged on and on, finally outlasting the kiddie lab. My judgment at the time was that finishing the book was more important than designing and conducting experiments in the red rug room. Perhaps I was wrong, but that was the gamble I took.

If I regretted that the experimental work fell so far behind the naturalistic, I had no one to blame but myself. It was certainly not Elsa Bartlett's fault. While I was off writing books and reports and visiting Chinese kindergartens, Elsa got the playroom into operation. She even read the book to find out what I had in mind. I once tried to acknowledge my debt to Elsa by calling the transcripts we collected "Bartlett's Quotations," but she laughed and declined the honor.

In my imagination, Year One was supposed to provide ammunition I could use in a campaign for funds to attract and support a more adequate research staff. The kind of naturalistic data collection that dominated the initial work was not good ammunition for my purpose; there is only so much playroom conversation by three-year-olds that anybody needs. But if we stopped recording and transcribing their conversations, what were we going to do instead? The more I thought about the kind of proposals I might submit for money to grow on, the more uneasy I became. Everything was taking longer than I thought it should have. As the year slipped by, my first bold confidence slowly gave way to misgivings about our direction and our prospects. By April 1974 my anxiety had built to crisis proportions.

If I had it all to do over, I do not know what I would do differently. But, oh, how I missed that intervening year of preparation. Has anyone ever written a treatise on what research workers should do when they get financial support before they are ready for it?

The Junior Faculty

"They named me Robin
Hood."
Jeff

I am sometimes asked why I decided to study three-year-
olds. The questions usually comes from someone who
thinks three-year-olds are already over the hill. I might have
worked with younger children except for two things. First, I
wanted their speech to be sufficiently mature that we could
transcribe it in ordinary orthography, without resorting to
phonetic symbols. Second, I wanted to avoid changing dia-
pers. When I asked my knowledgeable friends how old children are before they become both intelligible and continent,
the answer was three years. That settled it for me.

For Elsa Bartlett, however, that was only the beginning.
Elsa had to find the children, which meant finding their
parents. The search began with the Rockefeller community,
and all but two were found there. One of our criteria was
that the children would be able to attend from October 1973
through April 1974, and Rockefeller families could not only
guarantee that period of time, but could easily arrange to
deliver and collect their children. Via a communication net
mysterious to me, Elsa scheduled a series of interviews with
parents and their children and eventually selected eight
children—four boys and four girls—between the ages of
two years eight months and three years (between 2;8 and
3;0 in the terse but convenient notation of developmental
psychologists).

Since we were interested in the children's language, it
was important that they should be monolingual speakers of
English and both talkative and intelligible. Elsa went

through a picture book with each child to get some idea of perceptual and conceptual abilities, then talked to the parents and asked them to fill out a questionnaire about their other children, their own ages and occupations, and where they had lived before. And, of course, she explained the general nature of our interest and the criteria we were using to assemble the group.

For those parents with whom we struck a bargain, release forms had to be signed. This aspect of research with human subjects is seldom reported when work is published in technical journals. It is standard practice in psychological research to have experimental subjects sign a form that attests to their "informed consent" to participate in the experiment. Such forms usually explain the general nature of the experiment and the subject's part in it, grant him permission to withdraw at any time, and grant the experimenter permission to use the results for scientific purposes in return for a guarantee of anonymity. Our children were too young to sign anything, much less give informed consent; their parents' consent was required instead. Our form allowed us to make video recordings that we could use for teaching or professional communication as well as for research, and to administer standard psychometric tests to the children. Since the parents might not always be there in emergencies, we also got their consent to let us obtain medical aid should it be needed. Fortunately, this last permission turned out to be an empty formality, but you never know.

At the insistence of the Surgeon General, precautions of this sort have become standard in all fields of clinical research. Several years ago the Public Health Service got some very bad press as a consequence of certain ethically questionable experiments they had funded; they decided that if experimenters could not be trusted to police themselves, the federal government would have to do it for them. The dangers are greatest when surgical or pharmacological techniques are involved and therefore the regulations are written in strong enough language to cover such experiments, which sometimes frightens a prospective subject who has to sign a release form for a psychological study in which the possibility of injury would never have occurred to him if the form did not deny it.

The Rockefeller University has a special faculty committee authorized by the Public Health Service to review all research with human subjects in the university and to enforce acceptable procedures. If the university refused to comply, all federal support for research would be suspended, a threat sufficient to bring any university to its knees in these times. Consequently, every year I submit and personally defend to this committee a complete account of all the planned research in my laboratory that involves human subjects, along with sample release forms, medical guarantees, and assurances that the experimental experience will benefit those who submit to it. The relatively innocuous studies we undertake are easily defensible, but I must confess to amused impatience with being treated on a par with studies involving potentially dangerous techniques. Yet that is how bureaucracy works—in terms of general rules for all supplicants regardless of their special situations—and I make my peace with it in terms of its broader intent. Not all psychological experiments are harmless.

In any event, our eight children were protected against us, and we were protected against parental misunderstanding, by a system of rules designed to regulate far more perilous projects than we had in mind. One consequence is that I cannot use the children's names. I will, therefore, adopt a set of pseudonyms invented by Denis Newman, who worked on the transcripts with John Dore. The girls, in order of age, were Vanessa (2;8 in October 1973), Carol (2;9), Roslyn (2;9), and Nora (2;10); the boys were Marvin (2;10), Jeff (2;11), Don (3;0), and Kevin (3;0). Nora dropped out of the group after Christmas.

Our computerized transcripts have identified each child by the first three letters of the child's name, even when they were spoken to by name. The device is not perfect, however, for sometimes a name was spelled out or rhymed in conversation, and we have preserved the original video recordings where a determined snoop could break our code. (It is a bit like those exotic cultures where natives keep their true name a secret because they believe their enemies could use it to harm them.) But the general principle of anonymity for subjects is a good one, and we have done everything we could, short of destroying our data, to follow it.

During the first year, the parents brought their children to the playroom at 9:00 A.M. on Tuesday, Wednesday, and Thursday mornings, and picked them up again at 12:00. We chose mornings because children are rested then; an occasional afternoon session confirmed our prediction that sleepy children are fussy children, and hard to manage. Parents were free to stay and watch through the one-way mirror, but after the first week or so they usually left their child in Madeleine's care. By about 9:30 the group had settled down sufficiently for Elsa to begin recording the session. Between 9:30 and 11:30 she collected two reels of video-taped data each day. As soon as the video system was installed and working, we took the children into the recording room and tried to demonstrate how we were taking their pictures. They were little interested in our beautiful technology; they wanted to get back to the playroom. After a week or so they lost all curiosity about cameras that occasionally buzzed and moved, and went unselfconsciously about the business of teaching us how three-year-olds behave.

The room was so large, and the children so independent, that it was impossible to get a picture of everyone all the time. We coped with this problem by selecting a different "target child" each day. Wherever the target child went, the cameras followed; whomever the target child interacted with, the cameras recorded. By rotating the target child around the group, we hoped to obtain relatively complete samples of the speech of each child at regular intervals. It would sometimes happen, however, that the child selected as target for the day was in a surly mood and went off alone to play silently with some toy by himself. One of the lessons they insisted on teaching us repeatedly was that we should never take for granted what they were going to do. On the whole, however, the target-child strategy worked reasonably well.

One of the daily rituals was "snack time," when Madeleine gathered the group around a table and dispensed juice and cookies. Snack time not only assembled all the children in camera range together, but provided an occasion for introducing informal discussion of some topic of research interest. Discussion was sometimes interrupted by demands for food, and speech from a full mouth was not always as distinct as we would have liked, but snack time had the advantage of providing a group-centered activity without special rules about remaining in the group and participating in the discussion. Mandatory group discussions at other times raised disciplinary problems that were better avoided. I suppose that such tactical discoveries would be dismissed as self-evident by old hands at child research, and even by parents with large families, but for me they were a continuing source of enlightenment.

We had not entertained our young guests very long before we realized that they were an unusual group. In order to document our suspicions, Joyce Weil arranged for graduate students at Yeshiva University, as part of their training as school psychologists, to give the children intelligence tests. They did a beautiful job (at minimal strain on our limited budget) in characterizing each child's strengths and weaknesses, as well as in assigning mental ages. I have little faith in I.Q. scores in general, and even less for children as young as three; the actual numbers are not worth reporting. But the results indicated that, mentally, our children were nearer four or five than three years old. It was a pleasure to work with gifted children, but we certainly cannot claim that what they did and said is representative of the average child (whoever that is) at the same chronological age.

In addition to administering a standardized test, these student psychometricians also contributed insightful comments on the personalities of the children. On the basis of their short interviews they came to conclusions that we, who had known the children much longer, could only admire. Nora, for example, was judged to be a poised, mature girl, somewhat aloof. Roslyn was said to be generally quiet and shy, but excitable in speech, when her mind seemed to race ahead of her tongue. Marvin impressed the tester as a reserved, confident boy. Jeff was called a happy child, enthusiastic and cooperative, who answered questions carefully and thoughtfully. Don, too, was called a happy child, very self-confident, with a realistic assessment of his own limits. Kevin was thought to be somewhat tentative and dependent on the approval of others.

In order to get some better notion of their linguistic accomplishments, Katherine Miller, my patient and interested wife, agreed to compute the mean lengths of utterances (MLU) for six reels distributed throughout the six months we studied these children. The procedures for estimating MLU are spelled out by Roger Brown in his important book, *A First Language: The Early Stages,* but Kitty found that these children, who were more advanced than Roger's, posed a variety of special problems. The measure of length is not given in words, but in morphemes. For example, *walked* would be counted as one word, but two morphemes: *walk* and *-ed*. Roger counted catenatives like *gonna, wanna, hafta* as single morphemes, since that is how they must appear to young children, but our children were on the verge of saying *going to, want to, have to,* which suggested they thought of the catenatives as more than a single morpheme. It was not always clear where an utterance ended in our transcripts, or what to do about self corrections. And so on. After she had collected a list of scoring problems, Kitty wrote to Roger asking for advice. He responded with a long, detailed, and immensely helpful letter that must have taken him the better part of a day to write, and with this help she was able to score the transcripts in the intended fashion. The average MLU for all children in all sessions scored was 4.57 (4.66 for the girls and 4.55 for the boys), which put them just beyond Stage V on Roger's scale. Carol and Kevin had the lowest MLU's (3.12 and 3.17); the highest were Jeff (5.01), Marvin (5.10), and Roslyn (5.35).

The evidence indicated an increase in MLU (from about 4 to 5) between October and April, but the samples were smaller than Roger advises and I suspect that they were not collected in a situation where utterance length could be a useful indicator of linguistic competence. For one thing, children had to compete for the right to speak in the playroom; long speeches were seldom tolerated by the other children. An instructive example emerges from the data for Roslyn who entered the group with a particularly precocious MLU. In January she showed an MLU of 6.54 (computed for 127 utterances), but in March it was 3.88 (for 59 utterances) and in April 2.93 (for 14 utterances). I do not think for an instant that Roslyn was regressing linguistically; I think she was undergoing her first experience with the kind of treatment that the women's liberation movement deplores.

The boys dominated the group. They attended more regularly and thus usually outnumbered the girls; they were older; they talked louder; they showed more initiative in determining the group's play activities. Don emerged as a natural leader, with Marvin and Kevin as cooperative cronies. It says something about me, for example, that as I watched the tapes I did not see anything unusual about the social roles adopted by the boys versus the girls. But Kitty's count of utterances showed that the girls ranged from a total of 34 to a total of 241 utterances over the six hours sampled, whereas the corresponding range for the boys was 312 to 816. With this disparity numerically documented (and in the opposite direction from the common stereotype), I can now view the tapes through different eyes. There may be a moral here about the development of sex differences, and about the unconscious expectations of adults who let them develop, but I am not the person to draw it. The only moral I would draw is that very interesting results can be obtained from relatively simple analyses of this type of naturalistic data.

Madeleine, of course talked more than anybody. According to counts made by David and Nobuko McNeill, she contributed 42 per cent of the utterances; since her utterances tended to be longer than the children's, this meant that almost two-thirds of all the words spoken were spoken by her. In midyear I explained to Madeleine that we wanted to study child language, not teacher language, and she agreed to make a conscious effort to be more taciturn, but the statistics did not change—indicating, no doubt, that the demands of her role as teacher made it very difficult for her to say less than she did. There was a reliable shift in the children's utterances, however. Initially, more than half of their remarks were addressed to the teacher, but as the months slipped by they began to talk more to each other. By late spring, almost two-thirds of their utterances were addressed to other children—indicating, no doubt, their growing social skills.

To Madeleine and Elsa, each child quickly became a distinct individual with a name, a personality, a family, and a growing record of anecdotes and test results. All that came much more slowly and uncertainly to me, since I viewed the playroom activities from a supervisory distance and only participated actively as video operator on those rare occasions when Elsa was absent, or Elsa had to substitute for an absent Madeleine. I got to know the boys best. I could hardly overlook Don, whose father had explained my role and who thereafter addressed me with giggles as "Boss." I developed a special fondness for Jeff, a beautiful boy who seemed to me a little reserved but wonderfully imaginative. Kevin was slightly behind the others linguistically, which made me treasure him especially—he often taught us about the early stages of a learning process in which the others were already too skillful to make interesting mistakes.

I wish I could portray each child in all his or her uniqueness, but I see that even these feeble attempts draw me into invidious comparisons. I feel like a fond foster parent, unwilling to praise any one of my children over the others. Indeed, it would be most unseemly of me to do so, for I am deeply indebted to all of them for what they taught us, and to their parents, who so generously contributed the most precious component in our experimental plans.

Elsa felt that we should have held weekly meetings to discuss each child in detail, much as doctors present and discuss case histories of their patients. But the rest of us were too busy to attend, and only Elsa and Madeleine really knew them well enough to discuss them. In retrospect, I am inclined to think she was right. Not only would I have gotten to know each child much better, but I would certainly have increased the probability of my formulating some of those hypotheses on the basis of the naturalistic data that I wanted to subject to experimental test. But I decided to wait for the arrival of transcriptions that I could study before exercising my hypothetical faculty. By the time the transcripts arrived, however, the children had left.

Computers Take Over

"Kevin, what did you say?"
Marvin

Sexism is rampant in developmental psychology. If you try to list the most distinguished contributors in the history of the field, you will come up with about five men for every woman you think of. On the other hand, if you go out into the laboratories and centers where the research is being done, you will find about five women for every man who is working directly with children. These ratios are subjective estimates, based on my personal impressions, and perhaps they reflect nothing more than the difference between a sexist past and a rapidly changing present. But it is difficult for me to suppress an image of men riding into prominence on the shoulders of women who do the real work.

I have no delusions about who was doing the real work in the kiddie lab. Women did all of the supervising and testing of the children, and when it came to transcribing what the children said and getting it typed into the computer, the ratio was twenty women to five men. I feel helpless about such facts. Once I had secured support for the research, I had to hire people to do the work. When I tried to find people willing and able to do it, women applicants overwhelmingly outnumbered men. Should I have refused to hire them? That seems not only unfair, but stupid—in our culture, women are generally more skillful than men at these jobs. The most I can do at this point is to give them as much credit as possible and criticize a social system that pushes them into such roles. I dislike it—I think American children are overexposed to women—but I had to live with it.

I also had to live with my own mistakes, which was harder. I think I initially had a reasonable plan for learning to work with children, but my plan was derailed in the rapid rush of events. With respect to the transcription of protocols and their analysis by computers, I did not even begin with a reasonable plan. It seemed like such a cut-and-dried affair that it did not occur to me that a plan would be necessary.

Our original proposal to The Grant Foundation requested a minicomputer. I had some absurd idea that an operator could sit at the computer keyboard, wearing earphones and watching the television screen while typing the day's happenings directly into the machine. It must have been a very vague idea; just writing it down in the preceding sentence is enough to make me doubt I could ever really have held it. It is embarrassing to recall such fantasies, but candor is my objective. In this research I learned enough from my mistakes to fill a book. Maybe others can learn vicariously; it should be a lot less painful.

In any case, it quickly became apparent that two separate steps were required to get the children's utterances into a computer. The first was transcription—writing down with pencil and paper what the children did and said. The second was typing—putting the handwritten transcript into machine-readable form. Elsa Bartlett assumed supervisory responsibility for transcription; Peter Kranz eventually accepted comparable responsibility for typing. Both steps required far more time, money, and (mostly female) personnel than I expected.

The process eventually took the following form: first, Elsa previewed the more than about eighty reels of video-tape she had made and selected fifty-two worth transcribing in whole or in part. Then she and Madeleine assigned a tape to a transcriber who played it over and over on one of our two playback systems until it was reduced to writing. Next, Madeleine edited all of the transcriptions for accuracy while watching the television picture. The edited transcript was turned over to Peter and his assistants, who assigned a typist. The typed transcript was printed out by the computer and edited for typing errors. Since the quality of the transcriptions was highly variable, editing turned out to be no small task. Finally, the edited output was turned over to John Dore—it was available to all of us, but only John and two of his graduate students actively used it—for coding. Each month Peter gave me a status report summarizing which tapes were at which point on the assembly line. Although what seemed to me a small army of part-time help was hard at work, I had to look carefully to detect changes from month to month.

You cannot take people off the street, hand them a videotape, and say: Here, transcribe it. Transcribers have to be trained. Showing them how to operate the video playback was the simplest part. In the beginning we had rather hazy notions of what would be involved, but we eventually learned how to do it. Elsa (and later Madeleine) would show the trainee a completed, hand-written transcript as a working model, along with the list of conventions that we had gradually hammered out for recording both what was said and what was done. Each transcribing convention was discussed and illustrated in the transcript. Then the whole process, from playroom to computer printout, was explained and used to emphasize the importance of following the conventions exactly. (The first transcribers invented a dismaying variety of ingenious solutions to various problems; we had to standardize everything we could think of in order to make the work of different transcribers comparable.) Then they watched a video-tape together and discussed what they saw: children, classroom, equipment, and so on. (Subsequently, the trainees examined all of the contents of the classroom shelves in order to become familiar with the items that the children used and talked about.) When all this was grasped, teacher and trainee began to discuss what to do about parallel action, identification of speaker, speech by speakers on and off camera, and other persistent problems. Then the tape that the trainee was to transcribe would be produced. In her preview, Elsa prepared a guide for the transcriber, noting the footage at which to begin, segments to be omitted, segments to be transcribed in extra detail, any helpful contextual information, and the footage to end with. (Omissions were such things as segments of poor audio recording, an unintelligible babble of multiple voices, reading stories, rest time, playing music.) The guide was explained, and teacher and trainee worked together for a while: naming the children, noting idiosyncracies of pronunciation, and so on. After that, the trainee worked alone for a time. On the second day the trainee produced a short sample and the teacher reviewed it, correcting errors, misunderstandings of the conventions, misidentification of speakers, over-interpretation of events, misuse of punctuation. Madeleine later commented, "The biggest overall training problems were simply the decisions on how to break down and record simultaneous utterances and conversations."

I have described this training procedure in order to convey a feeling for why transcription took so long. It was tedious work—at least ten hours for one hour of tape—and some people were much better at it than others. We had a steady turnover of personnel; in our experience, transcribers who did not do good work after about a week never did and had to be dismissed; even those who did good work could not stand the strain indefinitely. Moreover, the video playbacks were not always working; time for repairs slowed the transcription schedule even more.

In my planning of the laboratory space it had never occurred to me to set aside a room for transcription. It had to be done in any empty room that was available. That usually meant the neglected red rug room, or the playroom and control room when school was not in session. Transcription went on sixteen hours a day, and transcribers had a tendency to turn the volume up when they could not hear something—which was most of the time. It is to the great credit of my colleagues on the fourth floor of the Tower Building that I received no complaints about the sound of children's speech filling the halls day and night; if they felt the same way I did, they must often have wanted to complain.

I was convinced that the transcribers would hear better and disturb others less if they used earphones, instead of the loudspeaker, but I was never able to persuade them, even after I bought the earphones and tried to illustrate my point. I was also concerned about frequent stopping and backing up, over and over; about the wear on both the playbacks and the tapes. Peter Kranz conceived and our electronic shop built a clever machine for playing the audio signal over and over on a continuous loop that could be slowly advanced, but nobody ever used that, either. I had to grin and bear it. I was lucky to be getting transcriptions at all; if they insisted on going about it in their own way, there was nothing I could do.

Converting the handwritten transcripts into machine-readable form was also a time-consuming task. The work included six basic steps: (1) typing the material into some machine, normally creating short files of 100 to 200 lines of text; (2) when necessary, converting this typed output into a form acceptable to the large computer that ran the text-processing programs; (3) combining a number of small files into one longer file for greater efficiency on the computer; (4) running the material through the computer as "pass one"; (5) noting errors detected by the computer program, proofreading for other errors, and writing the necessary corrections on the printed record; and (6) making the corrections and producing a new printout and corrected computer file on "pass two." Steps (5) and (6) usually had to be repeated in order to obtain a satisfactory level of accuracy.

Three different machines were used in step (1) for the typing: the minicomputer we had purchased initially with the intention that it would be used for all data input; tele-typewriters that we subsequently borrowed from Bill Estes's lab and from the physicists on the twelfth floor; and an old-fashioned IBM card punch. The minicomputer was by far the most elegant and powerful; it was located near the playroom; it was equipped with an editing program that enabled a typist to correct errors as they occurred. What I had not foreseen, however, was that the typing would be done on a part-time basis by a dozen different people. Donna Lyons, my secretary and an abnormally skillful typist, tried the computer keyboard and gave up in frustration. A small typing error could accidentally erase an hour of work, and new operators constantly lost material in the editing process. Since material frequently had to be re-typed, we tried making duplicate magnetic tapes before editing, but that also took appreciable time. Even when Peter Kranz did the typing, the facility to edit as the typing was done did not result in perfect copy, and the use of the minicomputer to edit the longer files was extremely inefficient. We eventually gave up on the minicomputer as an input device.

A teletype machine is much more primitive; it costs about a tenth as much as the minicomputer. It has the advantage of producing "hard copy" (the typed passage is visible to the operator), it is much easier to learn to use, and, since several were available, more than one typist could work at the same time. However, the output is punched paper tape and the possibilities for corrections while typing are extremely limited.

A card punch is about as easy to use as a teletype, and it has the advantage—because a card is easily removed from the deck—that corrections anywhere in the text are easily manageable. Moreover, in our case, a deck of cards could be read into the University's large computer much faster than the magnetic or paper tapes, which had to be converted. The disadvantage of the card system is the greater bulk of the cards that have to be stored. A card punch is not much fun to use, but it turned out to be the most efficient of the three methods of data input that we tried.

I am convinced that most laboratories go through such shakedown periods during which, by trial and error, they hit on the best solution to their particular problems. Not much is heard about initial misconceptions when the final product is published for public admiration, but these are fequently the problems you hear scientists arguing and comparing notes about when they get together informally.

What was the upshot of all this effort? The simplest way to answer that question is to reproduce a sample in approximately the form it was printed by the computer. I have taken one important liberty in the service of readability: computers always shout at you in capital letters and I have resorted to more normal lower case. The following is from a session late in the year, after we had mastered most of the problems of recording and transcribing.

April 4, 1974: **Tape one;**	1	
transcriber: Alice;	2	
children present: Kev,	3	
Mar, Ros, Car, Van;	4	
target child: Kev. Kev,	5	
Van, Car, and Jef at	6	
table painting paper	7	
mache animals. Jef not	8	
painting. Mar in	9	
background.	10	
Jef has paintbrush in	11	*Jef* Yeah an' I want it to
hand, looking at his	12	be a tall giraffe.
animal's head. Teach	13	
walks around table,	14	
behind Kev, toward	15	
Van.	16	
Kev looks at paint on his	17	*Teach* Well, I can't
arm.	18	change it, can I?
Teach moves Car's	19	*Jef* !I! can.
animal and wipes paint	20	
off her arm. Kev and	21	
Van look at Teach and	22	
Kev.	23	
Kev returns to painting;	24	*Teach* You can? How?
long pause during	25	
which all children	26	
attend to painting	27	
	28	*Kev* Hi Nessa
Van looks up at Kev and	29	*Van* Hi Nessa
both Van and Kev	30	
giggle,	31	
Kev points paintbrush at	32	*Car* Hi Nessa
Car, then continues to	33	
paint.	34	
Simult. with Car above.	35	*Jef* !Makin! it a jroff
Jef is looking ahead.	36	(giraffe), I'm !making!
He lifts left hand, palm	37	it a jroff. . .
up as he speaks. Van	38	
turns to face Car.	39	
Stands up and leans face	40	*Car* Hi Ne!ssa!
toward Van.	41	

Van smiling, facing Car.	42	*Van* Hi Nessa
Playfully exaggerated	43	*Car* I'm not !Ne!!ssa!
pronunciation. Car's	44	
mouth stays open after	45	
last syllable. Again,	46	
standing and leaning	47	
toward Van. Both girls	48	
smiling. Van begins to	49	
giggle.	50	
Jef rubbing face. Jef	51	*Jef* I'm !making! it a
swallows last word.	52	giraffe I'm making a
Teach walks toward Jef.	53	gira. . .
Kneels beside him.	54	
Van still looking and	55	*Van* Oh
smiling at Car.	56	
Again leaning with	57	*Car* No, no
whole body toward	58	
Van.	59	
To Jef. Van puts hand on	60	*Teach* Look, you know
wet point on neck of	61	what you do when you
her animal.	62	paint it? You can paint
	63	it a color. Then you can
	64	put spots on it and it'll
	65	look even more like a
	66	giraffe.
Van giggles. Faces Car.	67	*Van* Look. . .
Holds out hand, palm	68	
up, to Car.	69	
	70	*Teach* Okay? After the
	71	first coating gets dry,
	72	you put on another
	73	color for the spots.
Simult. with Teach.	74	*Van* Nessa
Leaning over to look at	75	*Car* Two spots eyes
Van's animal.	76	
To Teach, returning to	77	*Car* I got two spots eyes
own animal.	78	
Getting up and facing	79	*Teach* You do? !Oh!,
Car. Teach moves	80	how nice. I think you
finger in circle for "all	81	should paint it all over
over." Van looks at	82	green and then we'll

Car, then returns to painting. Teach walks away from table.	83 84 85	put eyes on it in a different color. Okay?
Teach closes door. Noises outside. Teach opens door again.	86 87 88	
Ros walks in holding back of her pants. Ros walks to table looking at others.	89 90 91 92	*Ros* Who just closed this door?
Teach closes door. Ros stands behind Kev's chair.	93 94 95	*Teach* I didn't know where you were gone so long.
	96 97 98	*Teach* Ros, do you want to play in the water table?
O/C Giggles.	99	*Ros* Ye-s. . .
Ros walks to sink. Teach takes apron from box.	100 101	*Teach* Here, put this on.
Other children watching Ros at sink.	102 103	*Ros* A little wa-ter?
O/C Teach brings apron to Ros.	104 105	*Mar* First, some, some, heavy water.
Teach whistles.	106	*Teach* Here Ros.
Teach sings her name. Teach puts apron on Ros.	107 108 109	*Teach* Ros.
O/C Teach goes to table to turn upright the water cup that Kev has just knocked over with his paint brush.	110 111 112 113 114	*Mar* See wan, wa, there's a lot of water and (inaud.)
To Kev, kneeling.	115 116	*Teach* Come on, come on.
O/C Screams to the word.	117	*???* S'hot!
	118 119	*Teach* You can't (inaud.) all the time.
	120 121	*???* It's sort of (inaud.)
O/C Teach stands up. Jef looking forward.	122	*Jef* When we watched

Teach comes toward him.	123 124 125	Sesame Street we saw a anteater, changing into a ger, a geraffe.
O/C	126 127	*Ros* (inaud.) need this, flip it out, scoop it up.

Van looks up at Teach.
  Kev lifting his head
  higher to look at
  Teach's face as he says
  "inside."
	128
	129
	130
	131
	132
		Kev I'm painting
		  !in!side.

Teach is standing behind
  Van, looking down at
  children.
	133
	134
	135
		Teach Fine.

Van mumbles.
  Quietly.
	136
	137
	138
		Van I'm painting out—
		Car I'm gonna paint the
		  outside.

O/C	139
	140
	141
	142
		Mar See, see there were
		  spots in.
		Teach Don't forget the
		  legs too.

O/C Children all return to
  painting. Kev does not
  look toward Ros.
	143
	144
	145
		Mar Wa, m, Ros watch.

Kev looks up at Teach
  who has walked
  behind Jef.
	146
	147
	148
		Kev I painted the belly
		  button.

To Van. Van looks up
  shortly and returns to
  painting.
	149
	150
	151
		Car Don't take mine!

To Kev. Banging O/C	152	*Teach* Good idea.

Kev reaches paintbrush
  into hole in back of his
  animal. Banging stops.
  Camera changes to Kev
  and Van.
	153
	154
	155
	156
	157
		Kev I'm painting, the
		  inside

Giggles.	158 159	*Kev* Look it, I painted the !out!side.

Kev and Van pushing
  brushes into backs of
  animals.
	160
	161
	162
		Car I paint !out!side.

	163	*Van*	!Out!side
Children begin to chant	164	*Kev*	Inside.
together. Chanting not	165		
related to movement of	166		
brushes in tail hole,	167		
though the activity	168		
continues.	169		

This should be more than enough to convey the general idea. It goes on and on, line after line, page after page, day after day. If you read the way I do, you probably sampled a few lines and skipped the rest—it is not easy reading. But if you really wanted to understand what was going on, you would have to read it over and over. We found that it was a good idea, when trying to work with any transcript, to play the original video-tape through first in order to get a visual impression of the various episodes.

The line numbers down the middle of the page are there for the convenience of the computer. Peter Kranz prepared the programs for editing and processing the text on the University's computer. The editing program relies on the identification of each line of output text by number. In order to specify a change, you cite the line number and write the appropriate command: change, modify, truncate, save, append, insert, replace, delete, save/modify. If the addition of new material on a line causes it to overflow the allowable line length, the program automatically creates a new line and inserts the extra material in the right order. The program prints the corrected text, flags certain types of errors that it can recognize, prints the new line numbers next to the corrected text, and stores the new file on magnetic tape. This method of editing proved to be relatively convenient.

As of June 1975 all of the transcribable tapes had been transcribed and reviewed, but not all of the transcriptions had been typed and not all of the typed material had been edited. The work limped along into 1976 and is still not complete at this writing, although 20,000 lines (about 40 per cent) are in final form. Someday the 1973–74 corpus should be available to interested workers, along with our classification of the texts with respect to quality of the original video recordings and the amount of editing we have been able to perform. (If people use the tapes, they should be willing to report errors to us; if people do not use the tapes, no one will care whether they have errors or not.) Although the total corpus is still incomplete, most purposes of the laboratory were served by making available "authorized versions" of four one-hour samples, one each from January, February, March, and April.

Peter also wrote programs to search the utterance portion of the files for particular words of special interest to each research worker. For example, if you asked for all the color words, the lines on which these occur would be marked in the printout and at the end a summary would be given by target word and speaker. A natural extension of this kind of processing, of course, would be to prepare a concordance of all the words uttered by each child. Peter tried this and found that such programs run very well with small samples of text, but he was unable to combine all the available text into a single file in order to prepare a complete set of concordances.

I must conclude this account by crowning it with a garland of ironies.

All the while we were struggling to reduce the children's activities to written form, another band of transcribers in Washington was struggling to do the same for President Nixon's tapes. We could sympathize with their technical difficulties, but the great public interest in those transcriptions and the issues surrounding them cast an unwelcome shadow over our own efforts. I remember being stopped on the campus by an intense graduate student in biochemistry who demanded to know whether I had considered the moral implications of my research. He was concerned that, by transcribing what the children said and did, we were contributing to a general public atmosphere in which such violations of a person's privacy would be accepted as natural and proper. I tried unsuccessfully to reassure him, and wondered to myself whether he might not be right. Everyone knows about the road that is paved with good intentions, but it is often difficult to know when you are traveling it.

A more personal irony concerned the imbalance between naturalistic and experimental research that caused me so much distress. I complained repeatedly that the group was not making enough use of the children for experimental subjects. When they replied that if I would hire them some research assistants, they could do more experiments, I said that the budget did not include salaries for research assistants. But the reason the budget could not support research assistants was that I was pouring it into the bottomless pit of transcription and typing. At the same time I desperately wanted to move in one direction, I was stubbornly headed in the other. I did not realize that I was saying one thing and doing something else. I felt that I had struck a bargain with Mike Cole and The Grant Foundation to collect extensive samples of child language.

It was also ironic that Elsa and Peter had the direct supervisory responsibility for all this work. It was one of those jobs where thousands of sheets of paper were shuffling through the hands of a dozen different people; making sure that nothing was overlooked, misplaced, or lost required constant planning and attention. Whatever other virtues Elsa and Peter have—and they are many—neither of them enjoys such responsibilities. But they took it in good humor, and did it well—because it had to be done. Fortunately, Elsa could share her work with Madeleine Dobriner and Donna Lyons, and Peter could delegate some of his clerical responsibility to Carol Ann Eisen and Mary Jo Altom. But both spent much time on these tasks that they would rather have spent developing their own ideas.

A final irony concerns a common idea about computers. The fear is frequently expressed that computers cause unemployment—that by doing more rapidly, accurately, and inexpensively what it took many people to do in the past the computer will eventually take over all the jobs. Our experience was exactly the opposite. We started with a computer, but in the course of time we supported a large number of talented, deserving (and mostly female) transcribers, editors, and typists. In the end it was the computer that was unemployed. Maybe someday computers will take over more of this kind of research, but for the time being there is still plenty of work that only intelligent human beings can do.

Conversational Acts . . .

"What those kids doin', Madeleine?"
Roslyn

Understanding the minds of children from a transcription of their behavior in a playroom is like seeing a world in a grain of sand and a heaven in a wildflower; it requires considerable exercise of the imagination.

Imagination is as important to a scientist as to a poet, but it is used and disciplined in different ways. In his delightful book, *On Knowing: Essays for the Left Hand,* Jerry Bruner once commented that psychologists like to set themselves apart from others who try to understand the human mind. We attribute a sort of objective purity to our own insights, perhaps to protect our claim to have forged a distinctive intellectual discipline. It amused Jerry, therefore, that in the pursuit of that aseptic objectivity the psychologist is just as dependent as any other thinker on subjective accidents, odd metaphors, wild guesses, happy hunches, and chance permutations of ideas that come from who knows where; Jerry attributed them to the left hand. The right hand contributes order and lawfulness, technique and artifice. The scientist's job is to effect an internal transfer of gifts from the left to the right hand—but so is that the job of the artist. Left hands, Jerry seemed to say, are all much alike and need to be more trusted; the right hand of a scientist, however, is very different from the right hand of an artist.

A scientist must trust his left hand, but I believe that left hands can be as differently trained as right hands can be. Scientific imagination must work on redundancy, on repeated patterns. Science begins by recording the most obvious and banal facts, classifying them, searching for patterns among them. It presupposes recurrences. Whitehead, in his *Introduction to Mathematics,* wrote, "The whole life of Nature is dominated by the existence of periodic events, that is, by events so analogous to each other that, without any straining of language, they may be termed recurrences of the same event" (p. 164). Unfortunately, events do not come with labels on them: "Look at me, I'm recurrent," or "Ignore me, I won't happen again." Indeed, they do not even come labelled: "I am an event." Such labels must be imposed on Nature by an observer. Until they have been, a scientist has nothing to work with.

What recurrent events can be observed in children's speech and behavior? A basic event is the utterance of a word; the recurrence of words in speech is fundamental to any scientific account of language. Moreover, words form recurrent patterns—phrases, clauses, sentences. Those, too, are fundamental to the science of language. Such recurrent linguistic events have long been recognized; we did not have to invent them in order to analyze what the children said.

Where invention becomes necessary is in the classification of still larger communicative events. In order to appreciate the problem, you must realize the variety of possibilities among which an analyst must choose. What about a conversation, for example? Is that a recognizable communicative event? If so, is it atomic or molecular—unanalyzable or analyzable into component events? Maybe greetings are communicative events—they seem recognizable enough. Or would you count the greeting and its acknowledgement as an event? Maybe the transcriptions should be broken down into ideas, into the philosopher's "propositions," and classified as true or false. Or perhaps an outline of the main and subordinate ideas could be constructed. A different approach might try to catalog intentions: what did the speaker intend to accomplish by saying and doing what he said and did? Intentions are obviously important, but are they recognizable enough for scientific purposes? Then there are a host of more mechanical alternatives: counting the relative number of adjectives versus verbs, for example; devising various indicators of sentential complexity; classifying intonational patterns used by different speakers on different occasions; looking to see where pauses occur; recording the order of speaking and who speaks to whom. You could even count the number of utterances beginning with consonants versus vowels, if you had some reason to think the results would be meaningful. Most of these various alternatives have been tried at one time or another, and there must be many other possibilities that have not yet been invented.

It is a problem of choice. What choice you make will depend on what you want to know; that, in turn, will depend on your notions about what is going on. Imagination is indispensable. You try to imagine what is going on, you invent units of analysis to test your idea, and you try to apply those units to the transcripts; then you sit back and pray for a gift from the left hand, something to tell you whether you should change your units or your theory (or both) in order to improve the match between them. It is a slow process, back and forth, until, if you are lucky, something grows weblike in your mind, a representation in which you hope to capture the children's behavior.

David McNeill tried to impose order on our recordings. Early in the year he hired a transcriber with his own research funds to search for particular conversational events, but when the transcriber had to resign, he did not try to replace her. He decided to rely on our transcriptions instead.

What he was looking for was dictated by results he had obtained the year before at the University of Chicago, where he had watched even younger children in group interaction with parents. Dave had found, for example, that the frequencies with which different types of remarks are made by children mirror rather closely the frequencies with which such remarks are made by adults. (There were some interesting exceptions. For example, middle class parents frequently ask children "test questions"—questions to which the interrogator already knows the answer, like "What is this called?" or "How old are you?" Young children less often ask a question of another child, but when they do, it is nearly always because they want to learn the answer.) In order to make such analyses, Dave had developed his own scheme for categorizing utterances of different types.

Since our sample of child language was considerably larger than the sample he had obtained from two-year-olds, Dave and his wife Nobuko were able to make extensive correlations between the types of utterances that are addressed by children to other children, by children to adults, and by adults to children. They found some evidence that Madeleine tended to adapt her own speech to the speech of the children—that she often spoke a dialect that some workers have called Motherese—but the overall pattern of correlations led them to question how important such simplifications of adult speech are in the total language experience of children.

These analyses by the McNeills were not carried out at The Rockefeller University, however; we had to invent our own coding system for the data. The burden of doing this fell on our friendly Irishman and linguist, John Dore. John profited from discussions with Dave about the coding problem, but his own solution to it reflected a different pattern of research interests.

John's imagination was stimulated by the general concept of "speech acts" developed by such philosophers as John Austin and John Searle. These thinkers were interested in utterances as acts—acts of asserting, denying, questioning, advising, warning, promising, and so on—rather than as expressing propositions suitable for logical analysis. For example, if someone says "The door is open," it sounds like a simple description, but in an appropriate context that same utterance could be used as a protest, or as a request (or even an order) to close the door, or as an excuse for not answering a question, or as a warning that the cat might escape, or whatever. In order to decide what act a person was performing when he uttered "The door is open," therefore, we must decide what his intentions were; that decision, in turn, will depend on such complex and intangible matters as the nature of the situation in which he uttered it and what we know about him and his addressee.

One's first cautious impulse is to say that judging a person's intentions is too subjective for reliable scientific results—Freud and his followers taught us long ago that even the actor himself may be unaware of his real intentions. But such caution, while admirable in general, need not blind us to the possibility of a more limited analysis of the manifest intentions expressed in speech acts. Speech acts are special in this respect; they depend for their effect on a listener's being able to grasp what the speaker wants his utterance to be counted as. The listener is sometimes mistaken, of course, and a speaker may have other intentions than those he is willing to make manifest, but if the system did not usually work reasonably well—if listeners were constantly at sea about a speaker's intentions—language would not be the useful instrument for social interaction that we know it to be. Moreover, the scientist is a competent member of the language community that he is studying; his considered judgments of the speaker's manifest intentions should be no less valid than the judgments of the actual participants.

The obvious way to determine whether it is possible to categorize a speaker's intentions is to try it and see whether reasonable people, working independently, agree or disagree. John drew up a list of speech acts, or conversational acts, as he prefers to call them. In order to determine whether they were recognizable in the children's speech, he needed transcripts of the children's speech. Peter Kranz pushed one of the January transcripts through all the editing processes ahead of the others—he called it "the authorized version" for that session—and gave it to John to work with. Subsequently Peter provided four such authorized versions, one each for January, February, March, and April. These provided a corpus of almost 3000 child-utterances-in-context that John could use to test and sharpen his theoretical intuitions.

I would like to recount the successive steps back and forth between theory and data, and the various transfers from the left to the right hand, that led eventually to the list of speech acts John adopted, but that is John's story, not mine. I saw enough revised versions of the list, however, to know that the process continued over several months. When he was finally satisfied, John explained his coding system to two of his graduate students, Maryl Gearhart and Denis Newman, who spent the summer of 1974 independently applying it to the transcripts. They agreed on their initial coding of 82 per cent of the utterances; after group discussion, Maryl, Denis, and John eventually agreed on the coding of all the utterances. But John felt that 82 per cent agreement between independent judges was high enough to insure that other workers could apply his coding system to child utterances with substantially similar results.

At that time the list contained six types of conversational acts: (1) *requests* for information, action, or acknowledgement made up 27 per cent of the sample; (2) direct *responses* to preceding utterances were 18.5 per cent; (3) *descriptions* of observable or verifiable aspects of the situation were 22.3 per cent; (4) *statements* expressing analytic or institutional facts, beliefs, attitudes, emotions, reasons, and so on were 13.8 per cent; (5) *conversational devices* regulating contact and conversation were 5.8 per cent; (6) *performatives* that accomplished an act simply by being said were 10.8 per cent. (Subsequently "conversational devices" was dropped and replaced by two types: *acknowledgements* and *organizational devices*.) The wastebasket—unintelligible, incomplete, or otherwise incomprehensible utterances —caught 7.9 per cent, and 5.8 per cent were doubly coded. Within each of the six general categories a variety of more specific categories were defined—in all, the list contained 32 different types of speech acts that these three-year-olds performed.

Of special theoretical interest are the performatives, since it was this type of utterance that first led John Austin to become interested in speech acts. A performative is an utterance that does not merely say something—it *does* something. For example, the sentence "I pronounce you man and wife," when said by a properly constituted authority on an appropriate occasion, does something: it performs the act of marrying two people. "I bet you a dollar it will rain" does not merely say something: it offers a wager. Philosophers whose principal interest in sentences had been whether or not they expressed true propositions found these performatives puzzling; it makes little sense to ask whether "I pronounce you man and wife" or "I bet you a dollar it will rain" express true propositions. According to Austin, you can ask whether or not these sentences are used "felicitously," and that question leads you into a specification of the conditions under which they succeed in performing the act they are intended to perform, but felicity is very different from truth.

John found he could distinguish five different types of performatives in the children's use of language: *protests* objected to the addressee's previous behavior; *jokes* produced humorous effects; *claims* established the speaker's rights by being said; *warnings* alerted the addressee to impending harm; *teases* annoyed, taunted, or provoked the addressee. It is relatively easy for an adult to recognize these various performatives intuitively, since he knows how to play the game himself. In order to reduce the process to a science, however, it is necessary to make explicit all the factors that enter into the adult's (or any other competent hearer's) intuition. Each type had to be defined explicitly.

For example, the rule for protests is:

Utterance U is successful in consummating a protest if both the speaker S and the hearer H believe that U is equivalent to "I hereby object to your A-ing," where A is an act that H has performed that violates some right R of S.

The act of protest is consummated only when certain relevant beliefs are shared. These beliefs are:

(1) H has done A.
(2) S has the right R.
(3) In doing A, H has violated the R of S.
(4) S wants H to cease A-ing.
(5) H is obligated to cease A-ing.
(6) If S had not protested, H would not have ceased A-ing.

If, for example, the hearer does not believe that the speaker has the right in question, then belief condition (2) is violated and the protest is not successfully consummated.

(Note that it does not matter whether the speaker actually has the right as long as the hearer believes that he does.) Conditions (1), (2), and (3) serve to distinguish protests from simple requests for action.

Is it possible to tell from transcripts and video recordings whether all these conditions are actually met? The clearest evidence that a protest has been consummated is the hearer's response to it—he stops A-ing, apologizes, or in some other way accommodates the speaker. To categorize an utterance as a protest, therefore, you must consider a sequence of contingent utterances and, sometimes, actions. For example, a protest may be challenged and the speaker may have to state his right explicitly in order to consummate the act, in which case several successive utterances have to be considered.

When a child says "Get off my blocks," it is usually not too difficult to determine whether all the belief conditions for a protest are fulfilled. The judgment gets more difficult, however, if the protest is indirect. "You're standing on my blocks," for example, appears to be a locative description. But it is a direct expression of belief condition (1) for protests. If the speaker and hearer both believe that all the conditions for a protest are satisfied, "You're standing on my blocks" will have an effect not ordinarily associated with a description.

The transcripts provided persuasive evidence that these three-year-olds not only distinguished clearly between protests and requests, but that they also understood clearly the speaker's intention when the protest or request was indirect. In addition to demonstrating their linguistic competence to produce and interpret the spoken (lexical and grammatical) forms, they also demonstrated a communicative competence that involved an implicit appreciation of such social constructs as rights, obligations, roles, and procedures, insofar as these are relevant to the performance and recognition of conversational acts. John concluded that the rules governing conversational acts cannot be simple extensions of the familiar rules of grammar because, unlike grammatical rules, they involve many nonlinguistic beliefs about the world and about social conventions. The study of conversational acts not only goes beyond the philosopher's traditional interest in truth; it goes beyond the linguist's traditional interest in the form and arrangement of strings of symbols. A separate theory, pragmatic rather than logical or grammatical, is also required in order to account for recurrent events that can be recognized at this level of description. And the children seem as precocious in mastering this aspect of linguistic communication as they are in mastering the grammar and lexicon.

On the basis of his earlier research on one-year-old children, John had proposed a two-sided theory of speech development. On one side were the linguistic (phonological, lexical, and grammatical) skills required to produce acceptable utterances; on the other side were "orectic attitudes," or intentions underlying the infant's attempt to communicate, either through vocalization or in other ways. Coordination of these two aspects posed a central problem, not only for the child but for any explanation of language development. The conversational act is simply the convenient unit of behavior within which to study the integration of these distinct components of the child's developing skills.

After working with three-year-olds (and being exposed to more psychologists), John added a conceptual dimension to his formulation. Some theorists feel that there is a competition between conceptually based, communicatively based, and linguistically based theories, that one or another theory must account for everything. John embraces them all, and assigns to each its special problems. Perhaps the conceptual representation of knowledge must come first, then the intention to communicate that knowledge, and, finally, conceptual and communicative skills are reorganized, under social guidance, into a grammar. Perhaps. But John's thesis is that no one of the three components can explain developments in the other two; the emergence of language depends on the three components jointly. John's theory has a place for everything, and everything is in its place.

Coding the children's 2,829 utterances into 32 categories was an enormous task, requiring both ingenuity in defining the categories and patience in analyzing each utterance, but it was not an end in itself. As someone once remarked, categorization is the halfway house to science. The real return from such an investment of effort is not realized until lawful relations are found among the categories. Work on the corpus continued after the initial categorization in the summer of 1974. Indeed, John, Maryl, and Denis are still working on it while this is being written; a complete account of their findings cannot yet be given, but I can at least describe some of the kinds of questions they went on to study.

. . . Episodes, and Tasks

> "And after you's going to
> be my turn."
> *Roslyn*

John Dore finds writing to be the best way to think. Many people, perhaps most, resist writing until they know what they want to say. That position is defensible, but I favor John's way.

I remember as a graduate student hearing a professor say that he never knew what he thought until he read what he wrote; with that distinguished encouragement, I soon became addicted to the written word as the best way to clarify ideas. It has the advantage not only of fixing my thoughts in a tangible form to which I can react—edit, revise, compare, complicate, or even discard entirely—but when I am through, if the process succeeds, I usually have in hand a document that can easily be turned into a publishable manuscript. And publication is important, both for professional recognition and for the growth of science—unpublished ideas seldom survive. I suppose you could write too much; if you did nothing else, you would run out of new ideas to think and write about. But most aspiring scientists I have known have tended to err in the opposite direction.

Because John Dore works this way, he was by far the most prolific member of the group I assembled to work in the kiddie lab. As a result, there are available for my present purposes four manuscripts by John, and one each by his students, Maryl Gearhart and Denis Newman. It is their work and ideas I am reporting, often phrased in their own words. I wish I could take credit for it, but my role can be merely reportorial. When they publish it in books and journals, of course, they will acknowledge all the other workers who share their concerns; my report will be more provincial.

Once the children's utterances had been coded, it was a simple matter to pull out all the speech acts of a particular type and study them as a group. The first type John studied was the children's answers to questions. This choice was motivated both by the relative ease of identifying questions, which have a distinct grammatical form, and by their relative abundance in our data. It seems a happy choice. Teachers, parents, and psychologists constantly ask children questions; anything we learn about how they answer should be valuable information.

The transcripts John worked with contained 779 question-answer sequences in which the question was addressed to a child. In only fifteen instances was the answer uninterpretable. On grammatical grounds the questions were divided into two kinds: there were 285 *Wh*-questions and 494 *Yes/No*-questions. *Wh*-questions (*what, where, which, who, whose, how, why,* and *when*) solicit information of varying complexity, from simple naming in response to *what*-questions up to elaborate explanations in response to *why*-questions. *Yes/No*-questions (which characteristically begin with a form of *be* or *do,* but which can be asked with rising intonation on a declarative sentence, or by echoing a word, or by adding tag-questions like *okay?* or *isn't it?*) solicit confirmation or denial of the propositional content of the question. The children gave three kinds of responses: there were 312 failures to answer at all; 311 answers that were appropriate and grammatically matched to the form of the questions; and 141 responses that were generally relevant to the question but could not be counted as standard or predictable. Failure to answer was frequent both to *why*-questions, perhaps because the formulation of an explanation was too difficult, and to tag-questions, perhaps because these were not always recognized as questions.

In many respects, the children's nonstandard answers are the most interesting; they provide clues as to how the questions were being interpreted and responded to. John listed the following conditions for *Wh*-questions: (1) The questions must be understood. A child who does not understand the proposition underlying the question may ask a clarification question in return: "Huh?" or "What?" Or the child may indicate a misinterpretation by answering a different question: "What do plants need to grow?" "They grow in this." (2) The child must accept as true any proposition that underlies the question: "What number are you making?" "I'm not making a number." (3) The child must understand that the questioner believes that the addressee knows the answer. Awareness of this pragmatic condition was indicated by such nonstandard answers as "I don't know," or more explicitly: "What is that?" "I know, a carrot." (4) The child must believe that the questioner wants the information that is being requested; otherwise, children feel no obligation to answer. (5) Either the child must believe that the speaker does not know the answer or, in the case of test questions, the child must want to display personal knowledge. (6) The child must be willing to answer, that is to say, must have no more pressing desire at the moment. If any one of these conditions fails to apply, the child will either fail to respond or will respond in some nonstandard way. Nonstandard answers also provided evidence for a similar analysis of conditions for answering *Yes/No*-questions.

Apparently, children do not feel obligated to answer questions—at least, they feel much less obligation than do adults. The effect is a certain unpredictability at the level of conversational interaction. One of the devices that adults use to regulate a conversation is the *Yes/No*-question, which generally has the effect of selecting the addressee as the next speaker, but the children were especially likely not to answer this type of question. John did not set out to study rules that regulate turn-taking in conversations, but his analysis of children's responses to questions raised important issues at this different level of analysis. When a child does not answer a question, does it mean that the conditions for the felicitous performance of that conversational act are not understood, or that the social conventions for turn-taking are not understood? In addition to integrating the conceptual, linguistic, and intentional aspects of a speech act, children must also master the tricks that adults use to regulate the performance of conversational acts in social interaction. The two levels of analysis cannot be unrelated, but how should their relationship be characterized? Apparently the transcripts must be analyzed into units even larger than conversational acts.

At the level of conversational regulation, theorists have identified such processes as beginnings, continuations, closings, qualifications, repairs, each of which has its own characteristics that signal how a speaker expects the conversation to continue. The techniques involved must be learned by anyone who wishes to participate in the turn-taking game that characterizes adult conversation. It was not initially obvious that such units of analysis are appropriate for the utterances of three-year-olds. For one thing, turn-taking presupposes the use of language for social interaction. At least one well known theory of child language claims that young children's speech is highly egocentric, that children do not generally talk to specified persons with the object of making them listen and understand until they are old enough (usually about five) to appreciate the other person's point of view. According to that account, our children were too young to be judged by adult standards.

Maryl Gearhart was troubled by this discrepancy between the well-known theory and her clear impression that our children did use language predominantly for social purposes. It seemed to her that a distinction should be drawn between using language with an intent to communicate and having the conceptual abilities required to appreciate another person's point of view. Some superficial devices can regulate conversational interaction—simple devices available even to children too young to construct an adequate conceptual representation of a listener's informational needs. Perhaps young children cannot use the full range of conceptual relations and logical implications that are available to an adult as part of the turn-taking system, but some of the more superficial signals may be at their disposal. If evidence could be found that young children use these simpler devices, one could argue that they are not being egocentric in their use of language, even though they may not understand the topical organization of the conversation in the same way an adult would.

Maryl decided that the simplest regulatory device to look for was the conversational beginning. A beginning turn in a conversation is relatively easy to identify. Whenever a new conversational pair is mutually created, the first utterance will be the beginning turn; special cases arise when a new participant joins an ongoing interaction, or when a participant begins talking to himself. She was able to identify about 250 beginnings in one hour of interaction. Some were beginnings by the teacher addressed to a child, some by a child addressed to the teacher, and some by a child addressed to another child. When she had classified all of the beginning turns in this way, she found that about 20 per cent of the children's beginnings were addressed to themselves, compared with about 2 per cent self-addressed beginnings by the teacher. Moreover, the teacher was clearly more skilled in selecting the person she expected to take the next conversational turn. Beginnings in which the speaker intended to engage another person were accomplished successfully more often by the teacher than by the children; the greatest proportion of failures occurred when a child tried to engage the teacher in conversation.

Since all the utterances had been categorized according to the type of speech act they were used to perform, it was a simple matter to compare the content of the teacher's and children's beginning turns. The teacher's beginnings were primarily requests—for information (48 per cent), action (22 per cent), or permission (2 per cent); the children's were primarily descriptions or statements (58 per cent), then requests (36 per cent). Requests are naturally suited as the first member of a pair of turns, but statements and descriptions do not demand standard responses. The teacher followed the conventional adult pattern in using requests as beginnings; the children, presumably expecting the same attention from Madeleine that they received from their mothers, more often tried to begin conversations with her with a speech act that does not demand a conventional response.

There is, in short, evidence for some egocentric use of language by these three-year-olds, but the major use is clearly social. However, they have not mastered perfectly the social art they are trying to practice. As Maryl remarks, her methods of analysis could be carried out for individual children over the period of six months for which video recordings and transcripts are available; the results would display in detail what individual children knew and how their conversational skills changed. Until she has completed that more ambitious project, however, we cannot go much beyond the general conclusions she reached in this preliminary investigation of a single hour of classroom interaction. Those conclusions are sufficiently pertinent, however, to reinforce the feeling that units of analysis longer than single conversational acts must be explored.

John's study of answers and Maryl's study of beginnings go beyond simple conversational acts—they deal with sequential pairs of acts—but both seem to demand some larger context for their interpretation. What should that larger context be? A conversation? Yes, of course, such pairs of conversational acts are fragments of interaction that, under ideal conditions, can be represented as conversations, with recognizable openings and closings. But to recognize a social interaction as having various conventional markings of a conversation does not tell us much about what the conversation accomplishes. John started his exploration of these communicative phenomena with an interest in speaker's intentions; that interest should not be lost from view when it is put into an appropriate pespective.

Denis Newman took a different cut at the problem. Once a fight broke out between two of the boys, an event so intense that it aroused Denis's curiosity. What caused it? In particular, could normal interpretive techniques applied to the transcripts provide objective evidence to indicate what had happened?

After viewing the whole session a dozen times and working extensively with the transcript, Denis selected a 16-minute segment for detailed analysis, a segment that included the relevent events leading up to the fight and subsequent events that resolved it. The whole segment represented something that Denis called an episode, extending beyond the fight and having a structure of its own. He commented that as the underlying structure became more visible to him, his interpretation of individual events changed and began to take their significance more from the structure in which they were embedded. And as events were reinterpreted in terms of the whole episode, the episode itself became clearer and encompassed more events and modified still further his original interpretations. As he worked back and forth between the data and his interpretations, the sequence of events took on a coherence for him that seemed to justify his treating them together as a single episode.

The immediate cause of the fight was disputed ownership. One child refused the other permission to play with a certain toy, and this refusal provoked a physical attack. In order to understand how this could happen, it is necessary to understand how ownership was established in this group. Once this social convention is clear, the next step is to discover how the children's use of it led to a fight.

Possession, even among three-year-olds, is defined by social conventions. A child who is playing with a toy thereby establishes transient ownership of it; among coparticipants the objects played with, as well as the activity itself, are owned jointly. Ownership persists as long as the play episode persists, and one of the rights that an owner enjoys is control over any nonparticipant's right to use the objects and join in the activity. For example, Don and Kevin were playing with three wooden boxes that they arranged first as a train, then as a diving board, and so on. At one point, Marvin tried to sit on one of the boxes. Don told him not to. Madeleine then asked Don to tell Marvin why he could not sit on the box, and Don said to him, "Nope, because we made this all by ourselves." The explanation established joint construction as a basis for joint ownership, and Marvin accepted it. Sometime later Don and Kevin left the boxes for other activities, and eventually Marvin began playing with the boxes. Noticing, Don, followed by Kevin, ran over to the boxes and told Marvin, "Nooo, I, I didn't, ah, we got that for Christmas." Although it was still the case that Don and Kevin had "made this" arrangement of boxes, it was recognized that this fact no longer established their rights following an extended and voluntary lapse in playing with them; the best Don could do under those circumstances was to display his determination by an imaginative but unreasonable claim of ownership based on the magic of Christmas. That time, however, Marvin did not accept the claim and continued playing as before.

So that is how that work gets done. Sometimes, however, it is necessary to publicize a claim to ownership. For example, if a child needs to leave a toy momentarily to fetch something, an announcement of what is happening can sometimes protect rights of ownership during the absent interval. Or ownership may be established by making the first claim: "This is *my* chair." Or a claim to the status of coparticipant and co-owner may be made by repeating with little change what the first claimant has said—Denis commented that such repetition was a pervasive feature of the children's verbal interactions.

The fight developed while Don and Marvin were taking turns playing with a grinder, a toy that only one person could operate at a time. While Marvin was taking a turn, Kevin, an outsider, asked "Can I try it?" and Don responded emphatically "No." Kevin asked "Why?" and Don responded "Only two men to do it." When Don then replaced Marvin and began his turn with the grinder, Kevin, his patience exhausted, shouted "No" and lunged forward to grab it. Don held him off with his left hand while continuing to grind with his right. Kevin began pounding Don's shoulder with his fists, but Don managed to push him away as Madeleine arrived. Marvin removed the grinder from its support and held it in his hands; Marvin and Don looked at it as Madeleine talked to Kevin, who was crying.

It took Madeleine a moment to understand Kevin's problem, since Marvin was holding the grinder while Don was exercising the rights of ownership by refusing Kevin access to it, but it was soon straightened out. Marvin handed the grinder to Kevin and, after Kevin apologized for starting the fight, the episode continued. Don helped Kevin attach the grinder to its support, and they exchanged the following ritual greeting (which occurred several other times in the transcript):

Kevin to Don: Hi Don.
Don to Kevin: Hi Donnie.

They both laughed. "Now it's *my* turn," Kevin said, who was now a coparticipant in good standing. And that was how the fight was resolved.

A thoughtful reader may suspect some circularity in this account. First, the children's utterances are used to establish felicity conditions for making and responding to requests for permission. Then these felicity conditions are taken as a basis for interpreting the sequence of events and utterances as requests and responses. How can a class of utterances count as evidence for their own felicity? In order to break the circle it is necessary to establish that conditions inferred in one situation are also applicable to similar situations. Since there were many instances of requests involving social conventions of ownership, this method of testing the inferred conditions could easily be applied. Moreover, it does not invalidate the formulation of the felicity conditions for such requests that a determined outsider could not be permanently excluded, since it was clear that Kevin recognized the participants' rights even as he attacked them. The account does not try to establish felicity conditions for starting a fight. Even if there were such conventions among the children—which seems unlikely—there were not enough recorded instances of fights to support any generalization. But there are many instances to support the claim that the children did observe rights of possession underlying requests and responses to requests; these rights and rules sufficed to integrate a long sequence of interactions into the kind of coherent pattern that Denis called an episode—in this instance, a sequence during which particular rights of ownership were in effect.

Presumably, therefore, episodes are the kind of larger units in terms of which speech acts, and sequences of speech acts, must be interpreted. Since analysis into episodes requires repeated instances on which to test one's formulation of the rights and rules that define them, it was natural to search the transcripts for situations that arose repeatedly. These are easily found. For example, there were periods of free play, snack time, story telling, and so on, during each of which different rules applied. Learning to recognize these different social activities and to behave appropriately in each one is an important part of a child's socialization. And each activity has its own complex episodic structure.

Most of the recurring situations in the playroom were dictated by the teacher, which led John and his co-workers to refer to them as "tasks." Each task is structured into characteristic phases. For example, when Madeleine initiated a period of drawing, there was an arrangement phase during which the necessary materials were assembled and the activity was begun, then a monitoring phase during which the children asked for help and Madeleine checked their progress, and finally a finishing phase during which the whole group discussed what had been drawn and hung the drawings on the wall. Tasks provide an analysis of social activity, not conversation, but the conversation that occurs during any particular phase (most of it, anyhow) must be interpreted in terms of how it helps to accomplish that phase of the social activity.

The program now facing John and his co-workers, therefore, is to sort out the task structures that recur in the transcripts and to identify normative principles that the teacher and the children conform to in each case. If they are successful, the results should be a set of appropriate social contexts within which the conditions governing individual conversational acts can be understood. Their initial attempts look promising, but much remains to be done.

At the time I am writing this, the children whose behavior is being dissected so patiently are six years old. All that remains of their contribution to the work are the flickering video images and the transcripts, but in that form our three-year-olds have become little Peter Pans, destined never to grow old. I like to imagine that by the time the real children get to college they will be able to study, in advanced courses and informative texts, the principles of human growth and communication that they taught us in the playroom. I hope we make it in time.

Make Believe

"I'm driving lots of crooked
ways and straight ways and
bumpy ways and zigzag
ways, following the sheriff
of Na, Na, Nottingham."
Jeff

I t is presumptuous of me—especially after illustrating how
carefully John Dore and his co-workers search for evidence to support their generalizations about what the children were doing—to offer any personal views about what
was going on in the playroom. The following, therefore, is a
deliberate lapse from scientific rigor—no more than one
chap's opinion. (But no less, either; hypotheses have to
come from somewhere.)

One aspect of the activities in the playroom surprised me,
and long experience has taught me to pay attention to surprises; they usually teach you something. I was surprised
by the unreality of the children's world.

What do I mean by unreality? Well, it *was* a playroom,
wasn't it? Elsa and Madeleine had seen that it was well
stocked with appropriate toys and instructive playthings. It
is beyond dispute that a toy horse is not a real horse. Nor is
a wooden box a real train or a real house or a real throne.
Moreover, Madeleine read them stories about imaginary
children. The blanket of unreality in which they were
wrapped is absolutely conventional and highly approved in
our culture. There is nothing surprising about it for any
socialized adult in middle-class America. You have to look

with the eyes of a man from Mars to see anything surprising about that.

But there was more. The children engaged in make-believe activities, either as spontaneous games or obvious fantasies. Frequently they imitated adults and practiced their conceptions of adult roles, even wearing adult clothes. Their ownership of the toys they played with was not real ownership; their paintings were blotches with wild stories attached to them; their answers to questions were often absurd, apparently deliberately so; they made up fictitious names to call each other. In short, they behaved like normal young children with highly active imaginations.

All of which is perfectly ordinary, so ordinary that it took me a long time to recognize how much of their world was totally unreal. My surprise came less from anything unusual in the situation or their behavior than from the jolt I felt in applying the word "unreal" to it. It sounds disparaging to call something unreal. I had been taught to value a firm sense of reality and to distrust anything that departed from it. To say that children are imaginative, that they like to play and make believe, is commonplace to the point of banality. But to call it a world of unreality helped me to see it in a new light.

Wise men have warned us for centuries that words are treacherous. One of the tricks they play is to hang values on their referents. For example, if you call a man thrifty, you evaluate his behavior favorably; if you call him stingy, the same behavior is evaluated very differently. One way to dodge this particular trick is self-consciously to apply both evaluative terms—the affective connotations tend to counteract each other, leaving the referent itself in clearer perspective.

I find this little strategem helpful in achieving objectivity about children. For example, the same behavior that is called helping in a play situation is frequently called cheating in a classroom. If you want to unclutter your view of what was really done, apply both terms and let their evaluative overtones cancel out. Or, to take another example, what might be called joking in one situation could be called lying in another. In most situations the evaluation that you assign has important consequences, but if you want to be scientific, you want to be able to avoid those consequences. In the present case, calling imaginative play unreal suddenly cancelled the connotations and gave me the eyes of the man from Mars—it let me see that the children were spending large portions of their time and mental effort elaborating non-literal activities, often in highly repetitive ways.

So I had finally seen the obvious. I thought it was important. When I tried to explain it, however, people looked at me with squinted eyes: yes, yes, go on, they seemed to say, waiting for me to get the point. I realized that I had not really seen the point myself.

It is in such times of confusion that Jerry Bruner has so often rescued me, so I tried telling him about it. Jerry's eyes, thank heavens, did not squint. They opened wide, and he picked up the ball as soon as I fumbled. It doesn't help to call it play, Jerry agreed. His word for it was "pretense," and he gave me a rapid summary of the role of pretense in cognitive development, starting from the earliest mother-child interactions. Long before they begin to talk, children extend whatever skill they are developing to a wide variety of situations, practicing it and discovering its range of applicability. When they explore outside the conventional range, however, it does not discourage or frustrate them; they enjoy it, laugh, and go on exploring. In short, they pretend, and the pleasures of pretense support their exploration of the world around them.

I listened with fascination. I had wondered whether the large component of make-believe that I had seen in our children was merely an artifact of the play situation we had created for them. But Jerry was telling me that this is the way children are, regardless of situation. Until they learn what is called reality by adults, they have no alternative but to live in a protective womb of unreality. Pretense is one of the ways they learn.

Perhaps this kind of learning is one variety of a more general process that psychologists call conflict resolution. Far too much has been said about conflict resolution for me to summarize it here, but a general idea incorporated into many psychological theories is that a person who recognizes two conflicting patterns in any given situation will experience relief and satisfaction from seeing the conflict resolved in a natural way. In various disguises this idea has been incorporated in otherwise diverse theories of cognitive development; much of a child's learning is supposed to consist of discovering how apparent conflicts can be resolved.

One might imagine that when children pretend, they are extending some new skill into inappropriate domains; they recognize a conflict between the pattern of the skill and the nature of the domain. If an extension does not lead to frustration, but can be consummated in spite of its inappropriateness, the conflict may be surprisingly and pleasantly resolved. All this is speculation, of course, and undoubtedly far too simple. But children do seem to enjoy such play—exercising some behavior appropriate to a car in a situation that offers little more than a wooden box to support it can be an engrossing activity for a young child.

Resolving conflicts is fun. Some theories of humor are based on conflict resolution; a joke may set up conflicting expectations that are resolved in an unexpected way. And, in one form or another, conflict resolution is part of almost every theory of esthetic experience; perhaps we enjoy art because, as Tom Bever says, it makes us feel young again—it reminds us of what it was like to learn when we were children, when learning was fun and vice versa.

So what is the point? One point, of course, is that psychologists should study pretense more carefully, should try to describe the mechanisms of and conditions favoring this kind of learning, and should, perhaps, determine whether the pleasures of pretense really are related to the pleasures of conflict resolution. That is what Jerry and other developmental psychologists he told me about are doing. On that point, therefore, I can do little more than wish them well.

It seems to me, however, that another point should be made: unreality is terribly fragile. It is like a bubble, vulnerable to any cruel stab from reality. I believe that one of the advantages bestowed on so-called advantaged children is that their bubble is usually protected long enough for them to master a more adult acceptance of reality. Anyone who hopes to prepare children to cope with the abstraction that adults call "the real world" must be concerned with the role of learning by pretense, and how best to exploit it while at the same time gently replacing it with other ways of learning.

That is one chap's opinion. I have no new evidence, however, that might move it along the road from opinion to fact. The unreality of the child's world was not what we studied; our target was lexical development.

Crisis

"I'm scared, I'm sca-a-red!"
Carol

The sap rises in the spring. They refuse to tell me who first applied that saying to me, but members of my laboratory have confessed that it helps them to accept my leadership in better humor. From my side, April is the cruellest month seems more appropriate.

By the spring of 1974 I realized that, after six months of operation, the kiddie lab was not working out as I had hoped; the fact that my hopes had been unrealistic did not make me any happier about it. The conflict between my desire to create a research unit focussed on the semantic aspect of vocabulary growth and my unwillingness and inability to do what was necessary to create and lead it was causing me severe personal distress. Formal experiments probing the development of selected lexical domains had not materialized. Computer programs to summarize the total vocabularies of each of the children had not materialized. Instead, we had accumulated eighty video tapes of playroom behavior and I was apparently committed to the slow and expensive preparation of transcripts that nobody but John Dore seemed to want. The more I contemplated another year like the first, the unhappier I became. One hundred and sixty video tapes of playroom behavior would only double a burden that was already intolerable. I wanted out.

I do not now remember what straw broke my back, but I do remember arriving at the lab one April morning in a cold rage, determined to destroy what I had spent a year creating. Since Mike Cole and I were in it together, I went first to see him. If he wanted to run the kiddie lab for another year, that was fine with me, but I had had enough. I had tried to collect the transcripts that we had told The Grant Foundation we wanted, and by now I had transcripts coming out of my ears. If he wanted to collect more of them, he could do it himself.

Mike saw I was upset before I got the first word out. He set aside his schedule for the day and gave full attention to me and my problems. He said that he certainly did not want any more three-year-old speech if I didn't. He was, in fact, well launched into an independent plan to collect speech samples in a variety of social contexts from white and black children of different socio-economic status. The recordings I had been making of the speech of highly intelligent, socially advantaged children were of little use to him for comparative research.

If I had not been so upset, I would have recognized that this was exactly the implicit message that Mike's absence from the kiddie lab had been giving me all year. At the time, however, I heard what he said only in the context of my determination to escape. He wanted the same thing I did, which established him as a friend and ally in attaining my freedom. He let me blow off steam and, when the time came, he took me to a small Greek restaurant on First Avenue and ordered lunch. I remember that some of the lab members came in while we were there; they took one look at me and started to leave, then reconsidered and sat down at a separate table. After lunch Mike took me to his apartment and poured me a drink. By mid-afternoon I was calm enough to see what had to be done.

In order to give the background, I must go back to late 1972. When I returned to Rockefeller in the fall of that year, it was approaching the time to request a renewal of a grant that Bill Estes and I had originally received from the National Institute of General Medical Sciences (NIGMS). Bill had assumed major responsibility for the grant in my absence and took the lead in preparing the proposal for the renewal, but Mike's and my interests were well represented. Since at that time I planned to move into the study of child language more gradually, my needs were modest, but the work I hoped to do complemented nicely the more formal approach that Bill prefers and we were all pleased with the package he put together. It was submitted in April 1973 and in due time we were visited by a panel of our peers who agreed with us that it was a good program of research. (I later learned through informal channels that are not supposed to exist that our site visitors had assigned our application the highest possible priority.) I was confident that I would have funds to support my research before the year was out. Meanwhile, the University agreed to support it until federal money became available, and I went ahead.

What we failed to foresee, however, were the consequences of the President's budgetary battles with the Congress. Those were the days when Nixon was impounding funds that Congress had appropriated, and he impounded us right out of business. When word came from Washington that our grant would not be renewed because NIGMS had no money for it, we were in deep trouble. Bill Estes and Mike Cole had other sources of support, and immediately set about finding still more, but I was left with nothing. It was some consolation that many distinguished scientists were caught in the same squeeze, but consolation will not meet a payroll.

Construction of the playroom facility was well under way by that time and I contemplated the prospect of leaving it empty until I could find money with which to operate it. At this point The Grant Foundation came to the rescue. Douglas Bond, the president, and Philip Sapir, the executive officer, were both old hands at the National Institutes of Health; they saw more clearly than we what was happening. Indeed, while Phil Sapir was at the National Institute of Mental Health he had helped to float many of the research programs that were being stranded by Nixon's tactics. They could not shoulder the whole burden, but they determined to use foundation funds to keep some of the more important projects running until the crisis passed. I do not know how important they thought our work was, but since they had just given us a research facility that we might not be able to use, they decided to keep us in the game for another round.

After a few phone calls back and forth we extracted those parts of the approved but unfunded renewal proposal that were most relevant to child research—some of Bill's and Mike's work and all of mine—and submitted them to The Grant Foundation. The Foundation, being free of federal red tape, could respond promptly, and within a few weeks we received $100,000 to cover our operations from 1 October 1973 to 30 June 1975. They made it clear that this was a one-time grant, not a commitment to a continuing program. If our work was not good enough to attract other support before July 1975, we could expect no further help from The Grant Foundation. Which was eminently reasonable, and more than generous. I feel a personal debt to Bond and Sapir that I can never repay, but if they ever ask me to do anything for them, it will go to the top of my list.

About $60,000 of that grant was for the operation of the kiddie lab; the unexpended balance of that $60,000 was the money that Mike and I had to decide what to do with on the frantic day I exploded. At this point I was willing to return it to The Grant Foundation if that was what it would take to extract me from the situation. Mike let me talk until even I saw that I was being silly. I was already committed to people for the coming year, people who had built their plans on the assumption that the kiddie lab would grow—or at least continue in operation. Elsa Bartlett had been appointed for another year; a graduate student had transferred from Columbia to Rockefeller in order to work with me in child research; Susan Carey wanted to visit us from MIT in order to use the facility; Joyce Weil, who shared my ambition to integrate the experimental with the naturalistic approach but was frustrated by my refusal to hire research assistants, had submitted her own proposals to the National Institute of Mental Health and to the National Institute of Education for studies in the kiddie lab; John Dore had submitted a proposal to the National Institute of Mental Health in order to continue his work; Mike and I had submitted a grant proposal to the National Institute of Child Health and

Human Development. Whatever my personal problems, I could not walk away from all that with a simple apology. Year Two would have to be devoted to digging myself out of the situation that Year One had created.

Two immediate steps had to be taken. One was to cancel the proposal that Mike and I had submitted to NICHD for funds to support some of his work and to expand the staff of the kiddie lab. The other was to talk to all the people who would be affected and explain that I did not want to continue operations during Year Two in the same manner as Year One. The first was simple enough. With Mike's consent, I told Carl Pfaffmann that I had changed my mind; he wrote a letter requesting permission to withdraw our proposal. The second was not so simple.

The most difficult conversation was with Elsa Bartlett. Elsa had poured herself into the kiddie lab; it was her creature far more than it was mine. But Elsa and I had had trouble collaborating. I think now that it was a matter of personal style. She did not act like the scientists I was familiar with. To borrow Jerry Bruner's metaphor again, Elsa had a strong left hand, but at that time her right was untrained in the technique and precision of experimental science. I did not know how to work with her and she, in turn, felt I was not providing the theoretical guidence she needed to interpret the observations she and Madeleine were making in the playroom. I had a strong right hand, but, where children were concerned, my left was a shriveled stump. We had never been able to get her left and my right coordinated properly, and our efforts had left bruises on both of us. The problem was how to tell her that I wanted to close her kiddie lab without implying that I was dissatisfied with her work.

In any case, I broke the news as gently as I could. I do not remember what I said, but Elsa tells me that I said I had lost interest in studying children, and that I wanted her and Madeleine to wind up the work by the following September. Remembering my agitation at the time, I can believe that I really did feel no further interest in any kind of child research—when I want out, I want completely out. Elsa took it well. She has told me since that she felt her only real failure was not getting me sufficiently interested and involved in the work.

I was on the verge of closing my personal postgraduate School of Developmental Psychology, and without that interest to motivate me, I had little desire to keep the kiddie lab operating. My personal need for the kiddie lab, however, was not the only factor that had to be considered. Others were counting on it, as Joyce Weil soon made me aware.

My conversations with Joyce were more pragmatic and less emotional, and led to a number of decisions that eventually governed our operations in Year Two. My sudden loss of nerve put Joyce in a professional bind—she had already submitted two proposals (which were eventually funded) for methodological and longitudinal studies of children's conception and language of time. Her idea was to combine the sort of experimental studies of semantic development that I was interested in with the kind of naturalistic observations of behavior-in-context that Mike Cole was interested in—and thus to provide an example of how Mike's approach and mine could be drawn together. She had the idea, which I encouraged, that if she compared children's time language in different situations—one-to-one experiments, covert experiments in a playroom disguise, and spontaneous speech—she might find that the same children who seemed to know particular temporal words in one context might fail in other contexts. She suspected that middle-class white children in our playroom would show fewer differences as a function of context than would disadvantaged black children in a Harlem day-care center. It was an ambitious project, but one that promised results of considerable practical importance.

Joyce did not want to withdraw her proposals just because I was withdrawing mine, so she proposed a compromise. If I would allow her to use the playroom and would pay the salary of a teacher, she would assemble the groups of children she needed and would pay her own research assistants, and the kiddie lab would continue for another year. Her proposal amounted to a direct reversal of the decision I had just made to close the kiddie lab, but I eventually accepted it. My initial anger was fading and I was finding it increasingly difficult to be unreasonable. There was enough money in the budget to pay a teacher; Joyce needed the playroom facility and she promised not to bother me with the details of running it. I reconciled myself to the arrangement with the thought that everything, even stopping, took longer than it should have. At least it respected my personal desire to withdraw.

In order to save some of my intention, however, I insisted on a couple of reservations. Joyce agreed that her assistant would collect some data for Elsa on the children's knowledge of color and spatial terms. She promised she would not video-tape every session, but would distribute it selectively through the year. And she promised she would take care of any transcription and typing that she required.

These were minor accommodations necessary to meet the immediate demands of the situation. My central point was accepted—Year Two was to be the final year for troops of children to invade the laboratory every morning. The fact that available funding would run out at the end of the year seemed to put that point beyond argument. Their effect, however, was to create in Year Two a more even balance between naturalistic and experimental work than in Year One—a balance that was essential to the integration of the two approaches that Joyce envisioned.

At another level, a dream was sacrificed: I stopped thinking of how the kiddie lab might grow to half-a-dozen staff members. I thereby avoided the prospect of providing administrative and intellectual leadership for such a group, a responsibility I knew I would discharge resentfully. Emotionally, I relieved my anxiety about proposing experiments worthy of large sums of money and reduced my guilt about not participating more actively in the design of experiments and collection of data, in return for which I accepted the depression of failure and defeat. Henceforth we were no longer laying the foundations for more ambitious projects to come; we were cleaning up the jobs to which we were already committed and trying to bring the enterprise to a reasonably dignified conclusion.

The conversations with Elsa and Joyce were the critical

ones, since they were actively involved in the operation of the playroom and the red rug room. Madeleine Dobriner was upset, but then agreed to continue as playroom supervisor for another year. John Dore already had enough transcripts to keep him profitably engaged for several years. Peter Kranz would continue to improve the computer programs and to process the transcripts. Dave McNeill was no longer actively involved; Bob Jarvella and Keith Stenning were sympathetic and, I think, relieved. My temper tantrum did not destroy the world, not even the part I swung at.

Thus, the crisis passed. But we entered Year Two in a very different spirit from that which had inspired Year One. As it worked out, I did not even close my personal postgraduate School of Developmental Psychology. Events in Year Two kept me interested in the topic in spite of myself.

Year Two

"Let's all stick together."
Marvin

Once I abandoned hope, formal experiments began to materialize. Perhaps the violence of my withdrawal persuaded everybody that I had been serious about wanting them, but I think they would have materialized anyhow if I had been willing to wait patiently for events to unfold. The groundwork for them had already been laid. I find it difficult to develop any general theory of leadership adequate to my own experience.

In Year Two Joyce Weil assumed the responsibilities that Elsa Bartlett had borne in Year One. Joyce is an excellent administrator, in the sense that she can assess a task quickly, divide it into a list of subtasks that can be assigned to different people, and keep track of where each person is and what help they need. During the first year Joyce had chafed under what she viewed as my spineless approach to administrative decisions and my grateful reliance on others to keep track of things. It had been seven years since Joyce had administered a large research program at City University and she was not eager to go back to such chores. It was all so easy for her that she had to resist it like temptation; indulging her organizational talents could make her wonder why she wanted to be a psychologist. But the kiddie lab had become a challenge to her. She could spend only part time at Rockefeller, but she wanted to prove a point.

Which she did. An important reason it seemed simple for Joyce was Mary Jo Altom. The first thing Joyce did with the funds she received from the National Institute of Education was to hire two research assistants. One was to help Joyce translate the theoretical ideas into tests that could be given to children. The other was Mary Jo, who was to give the tests to children in the kiddie lab. Actually, Mary Jo contributed a great deal more than testing.

Graduate students at Rockefeller, relative to most universities, are reasonably well supported—a Harvard friend of mine once referred to them as "the fat cats of American graduate schools." By absolute standards, however, they are still close to the poverty line; New York is an expensive city. Only monastic devotion to study and research can prevent our students from resenting that they cannot afford to do anything else. If you are married, your spouse can work and supplement the family income; if you are married and have children, your student stipend is pathetically inadequate. The Altoms were married and had a son.

Mark Altom was a graduate fellow working in Bill Estes's lab. In October 1973, when Elsa began recruiting children, Mark and Mary Jo entered their son in our play group. This brought Mary Jo to the lab and gave her some free time. Since Peter Kranz needed helpers to type and edit transcripts, it was not long before Mary Jo was on the payroll part-time. Peter quickly discovered she had a good head and was willing to work. With the help of an elaborate mosaic of baby-sitting arrangements, Mary Jo found time to relieve Peter of some of his clerical chores and free him for the programming that he greatly preferred. Mark, too, became interested in the work of the kiddie lab; together, the Altoms were important members of our extended research family.

My secretary, Donna Lyons, knew Mary Jo and recognized her ability. At Donna's suggestion, Joyce, with only momentary qualms, set out to steal her away from Peter in September. When Mary Jo accepted the offer and Peter did the gentlemanly thing, Joyce's plans for Year Two were set.

The first responsibility delegated to Mary Jo was to assemble the groups of children to be studied. In the fall she produced three groups of different ages, each of which visited the playroom one day a week. As a member of the fragile subculture of parents-in-graduate-school, Mary Jo knew where to look for children and where to post announcements; the whole matter was accomplished with maximum efficiency. Joyce had promised that I would not be bothered with the details, and I was not. Since I did not go out of my way to meet the new junior faculty—I was already thinking of the kiddie lab in the past tense—all these children remained nameless strangers to me. It sufficed that Mary Jo and Madeleine knew them. But I was vaguely aware that the number of children we were studying longitudinally had been significantly increased.

Before Year Two could really begin, however, Joyce had to scale a mountain of preparations. First, she drew up a table with rows for various concepts people were interested in and columns for various methods of investigating them. This was presented to the collected members of the lab and, after group discussion, ticks were placed in the cells that seemed most important. After a little reorganization, plans emerged for five studies. One was to continue testing the children's production and comprehension of color terms. A second was to initiate her own tests of their production and comprehension of time words, plus some explorations of both verbal and nonverbal imitation. A third, somewhat vaguer than the first two, was to study deixis of time, that is to say, to study the children's ability to order events relative to the present moment, *now*. Study four was a continuation of tests of spatial ordering. And the fifth was to be a study of the children's number knowledge, because we knew that the time line and the number line are conceptually so similar. No one understood better than Joyce what ambitious plans had been projected, but she set about implementing them with spirit and determination. The five studies did not emerge in quite the tidy way this description of our planning might suggest, but, one way or another, all of them left traces on the eventual program.

During the summer of 1974, with support from her NIMH grant, Joyce collected a group of children in the playroom and began to learn how to operate the video equipment and to develop a battery of tests and experimental procedures that she could use in the fall. That is to say, during the summer she had to do the kind of tooling up for time studies that Elsa had already done for space and color studies. She had many ideas for getting at the children's temporal concepts, but she still had to discover which tasks were appropriate to different ages and what kind of data they yielded. And what kind of conclusions the data might support.

One of the more arcane aspects of psychological research is called the design of experiments. More accurately, the design of experiments is a topic in the study of statistics, but planning an experiment in such a way as to yield the maximum amount of reliable information is such an important part of psychological research that all graduate students (and many undergraduates) have to master at least the rudiments of it. Most psychologists become expert only in those designs they use repeatedly in their own work, a situation that lends some inertia to movements from one line of research into others. Longitudinal studies, for example, require a different kind of experimental design from cross-sectional studies. We were all more familiar with cross-sectional designs; getting our heads working in longitudinal ways took time. It was an additional source of delay in mounting experimental studies in the kiddie lab.

Some experiments are intended to measure particular quantities; these are usually called experiments in parameter estimation. Suppose, for example, that we wanted to determine how many times a list of words must be presented before a person can repeat it perfectly from memory. Our experiment would test several people; the average number of presentations required would be the parameter estimate, and some indication would be given of the variability around the average (the "probable error of measurement"). This particular parameter, however, would not be very interesting in and of itself. We can be reasonably certain that its value would differ for different conditions: for different items on the list, different lengths of list, different methods of presentation and recall, different types or ages of people, and so on. We can easily think of conditions that might affect the measured average. If we wanted to develop a theory of this kind of learning, we would necessarily make assumptions about what conditions do and what conditions do not affect it, and in what direction. In many fields of psychology, therefore, we are less interested in the exact value of a parameter than in the conditions that affect it—in this case, the conditions for optimal learning.

Testing such ideas requires a different kind of experimental design, usually called hypothesis testing. In its simplest form, two groups of subjects are tested: an experimental group, which has some property or has received some treatment about which we have a hypothesis, and a control group, which has not. If we obtain a difference in the predicted direction between the two groups, we would like to claim that the data support our hypothesis. But before we can be confident that the difference is not a consequence of random fluctuations, we must determine whether it is two or three times as large as the probable error of measurement. The larger it is, relative to the error variance, the more confident we can be that the observed difference was not a matter of chance variability—that it could be replicated if we (or anybody else) conducted the same experiment again. According to the logic of experimentation, such experiments can never prove conclusively that a difference is real; they can only make it seem highly improbable that the difference is not real. But highly improbable is not the same as impossible. When a psychologist says that his results are "significant," therefore, he does not usually mean what a layman would mean; he means that they can be replicated, that if the experiment were conducted 100 times, it should give the same result at least 95 times (or 99 times, depending on the "level of significance" the experimenter has chosen). The probability of successful replication has to be stated as a qualification to every experimental conclusion.

It is inefficient, however, to conduct a separate experiment for every condition that might affect a measured result. Moreover, some conditions interact. That is to say, condition A may produce one effect under condition B1 and a different effect under condition B2. The only way to discover such interactions is to test both conditions in the same experiment. It is at this point, where a variety of hypotheses are to be tested simultaneously, that careful experimental design is absolutely essential. The details need not concern us here. I have already said more than enough to indicate that there *are* details, that they are reasonably complicated, and that they are important. Experimental design is a technical subject.

In cross-sectional experiments, you are generally comparing two or more different groups of children at different chronological ages (or, in some cases, at different mental ages). In more complicated designs, you may compare children from two different social or educational backgrounds at several ages. It is important to match the groups in all relevant respects other than those you are trying to study; the problem is to know in advance what other respects are relevant.

In longitudinal experiments, on the other hand, you are generally comparing the same group of children with themselves at different ages. The problems of matching groups disappear in this situation, but they are replaced by problems of matching test materials. If you give exactly the same test a second time, the children may do better than they would have if they had not been tested the first time—either because they remember the test items, or because being tested led to interest in and learning about the material tested, or both. It is important to have test materials that are different, but that are equal in difficulty and that test the same abilities.

To establish empirically that two sets of test materials are truly equivalent is a difficult art in itself. Since there was not time for refinements, we relied on plausibility. For example, a child at one time might be asked to "Pat the horsie after you pick up the kitten" and then, at the next assessment, to "Pick up the pencil after you touch your nose." We would regard these two instructions as equivalent tests of the child's knowledge of *after*—more precisely, of understanding sentences of the form *B after A*—although some of the component tasks in these conjoined sentences might have been easier or more interesting than others. In order to control for such possible differences in the component tasks, they were combined in different ways, haphazardly, for different children—in that way, any differences should cancel out in the long run. But just to make sure, Joyce gave two tests of each connective, and when errors occurred they were not corrected by the interviewer.

Any likelihood that the children's performance improved because they remembered specific test questions was further reduced by the variety of questions that were asked: about color, space, and time. Too much testing, however, introduces its own complications. Children can be persuaded for a while that they are playing interesting games, but eventually they catch on. How they will react is unpredictable. Some will keep up a pretense of having fun, others will quickly get restless and want to go back to the playroom. One child, having mastered the art of playing such games, announced one day that *she* was going to be the teacher, and proceeded to put Mary Jo through an amusing series of pointless questions. Mary Jo was skilled in keeping the children's attention, but sometimes it was difficult to decide whether a child's mistakes were the result of a lack of ability or a lack of interest. Test sessions with an individual child might run anywhere from five to twenty minutes, depending on the number of tests the child was ready for, with breaks at any sign of fatigue or boredom.

Beginning in the fall, therefore, Joyce and Elsa were ready with some experiments to conduct in the red rug room (and also with some naturalistic tasks for Madeleine to introduce in the playroom), but many of Joyce's temporal tasks had to be pilot-tested the week before, and revised the day before, Mary Jo gave them the first time. The experimental battery that eventually emerged was given four times during the year. It was sufficiently long that it had to be spread over a period of eight weeks, at which point it was time to start over again. As the year wore on and the children became test-wise (and bored), the schedule was lightened a bit; not every test was actually given four times. The same tests were given to all three groups: to six children initially between 2;4 and 2;8, four between 2;10 and 3;1, and five between 3;7 and 4;0, which, for convenience, we came to call the twos, the threes, and the fours. The twos came in two days a week; the threes and fours only one day each.

The best way to give a feeling for the regimen that the

children (and Mary Jo) endured is to outline one cycle of tests that a typical child was given:

Week 1: Questions about long and short objects. Nonverbal imitation of sequences of two acts, in the forward order.

Week 2: Name six color samples. Nonverbal imitation of sequences of two acts, in backward order. Questions about first and last in an ordered spatial array. Act out temporally conjoined sentences in the imperative mood.

Week 3: Act out more imperative sentences with different temporal connectives. Arrange objects with intrinsic fronts in a parade. Act out more imperative sentences with still different temporal connectives. Name five different color samples.

Week 4: Act out temporally conjoined sentences in the indicative mood. Point to one of six color samples named by experimenter. Act out more indicative sentences with different temporal connectives. Questions about front and back. Act out illogical sentences in temporal order (e.g., "Put the doll's shoes on before you put her socks on").

Week 5: Point to one of five different color samples named by experimenter. Act out more illogical sentences with temporal connectives.

Week 6: Word association test using time terms. Arrange color samples in sequence. Questions about number concepts (e.g., naming numerals, counting, bigger and smaller numbers). Comprehension of questions beginning "when" or "where."

And so on. After eight weeks the schedule started all over again. It is a tribute to Mary Jo that she could truthfully say the children volunteered to leave the playroom in order to play these games with her.

All of that went on in the red rug room. At the same time Madeleine was providing data in the playroom. Joyce limited the video recording to eight sessions of each group (once each month through the school year), usually at snack time, when Madeleine could introduce an appropriate topic of conversation to elicit time words from the children. For example, in one week with the youngest group she discussed clocks and watches, with the middle group, birthdays, and with the oldest group, ages and counting; in subsequent weeks, these topics were rotated among the groups. All of this was recorded with the television equipment and subsequently transcribed. Sometimes Madeleine herself made audio recordings of the children's conversation with a small tape recorder, and those, too, were subsequently transcribed. And she carried out tests for Elsa of the children's memory for color; of their ability to answer questions about the colors of lemons, snow, blood, grass, and the like; of their understanding of the superordinate term *color*; of ability to place objects in front or in back of target objects; of their memory for a story containing temporal connectives; and so on and on.

I did not even try to keep track of what Joyce was doing with children in Harlem, or the several other research projects she initiated with her students at Yeshiva. I knew that she and Elsa had turned the kiddie lab into a data factory, but it is only now, as I review all that was attempted, that I begin to appreciate the factory's output. I had called for formal experiments. Year Two yielded more of them than any of us knew what to do with.

What we have inherited from Year Two is several office files full of data, much of of it still unanalyzed at this writing. Unfortunately, data analysis has proved difficult. Statistical niceties are almost impossible to satisfy; with just fifteen children, only the most dramatic differences can be shown to be statistically significant. The test results are enormously suggestive of hypotheses, but which results could be replicated, and hence are worth speculating about, is itself too often a matter for speculation.

I suggested to Joyce that, since statistical significance looked so problematic, it might be possible to develop arguments based on the plausibility of coherent interpretations of the behavior of individual children. Case studies, in short. When computer specialists try to program a computer to simulate some cognitive process, they sometimes begin with a detailed record of the performance of a single person. Then they try to write a program for the computer that will cause it to make exactly the same responses on the basis of a few simple rules. When they have it right for one person, they may try to use a similar strategy on a second. If the rules seem plausible and the simulation is enough like the human data that it is difficult to tell them apart, the model is generally taken to be a serious contribution—at least by those who pursue such research—in spite of a total lack of any statistical evidence of "goodness of fit" of the model to the data. Reasoning by analogy, I thought we might be able to formulate minitheories for each child by some clever combination of computer formalisms and clinical insights.

Joyce accepted my suggestion and pushed ahead on the assumption that I knew what I was talking about. When standard methods of statistical induction ran into difficulties, therefore, she fell back on her ace in the hole. From her perch atop mountains of data, she asked me to show her how to formulate a minitheory for an individual child. It was not one of my better moments. I have had some experience in thinking about such models, but I am unable to use it with Joyce's data. For a given child at one testing session, she had a little data about a wide range of behaviors—not enough data to develop a detailed model for any one task, and too many different tasks to be subsumed under any single model that I could think of. But even if I could formulate a model for one testing session, I have no idea how to formulate one that would allow for learning and development from session to session. When I realized that this exercise would have to be repeated for fifteen children, I looked at my crowded schedule and lamely confessed that my suggestion had been impractical. Joyce left my office feeling that I had let her down—as indeed I had—and determined to develop her own methods of analysis—as indeed she did.

Elsa Bartlett, relieved of responsibility for the day-to-day operation of the playroom and reinforced by the availability of Mary Jo and Madeleine to collect data for her, settled into the role of a research scientist. She still assumed some responsibility for supervising transcription of the tapes made in Year One, but that left plenty of time for her own work. She read voluminously, including, among other things, every book and article she could find on color terms and how children learn them. She planned her data collection more carefully and devised interesting ways to analyze the results. I left her alone and she set her own goals. The goal she chose was to produce some good science. Nothing could have pleased me more.

The kiddie lab maintained about the same size in Year Two. On the minus side, Bob Jarvella spent most of the year in Germany, but he had not been directly involved in the kiddie lab. On the plus side, Susan Carey became an adjunct member of the lab and began commuting from M.I.T. to Rockefeller. Sue had a particular idea for an experiment that could only be conducted in a longitudinal context— more about that, and Elsa's role in it, later—but beyond that she was interested in everything we were doing and willing to tell us about everything she and her colleagues at M.I.T. had been doing. She injected an air of enthusiasm that I badly needed after my loss of confidence.

Before the year was out, Keith Stenning and Mark Altom swelled the ranks of those active in the kiddie lab. Keith finally managed to reach closure on his thesis research and was at loose ends for his next project. After conversations with Joyce he decided to test children's short-term memory for the kind of sentences that Joyce was asking them to act out. Mark and Joyce conducted a carefully designed experiment on children's ability to remember sequences of illuminated pictures in temporal order or according to spatial position. Moreover, Joyce began bringing graduate students from Yeshiva to work at Rockefeller—many of our transcribers and editors were recruited in that way. And she persuaded some of them to conduct cross-sectional studies of temporal concepts in children outside the laboratory, as supplementary information to guide her longitudinal study.

In short, the kiddie lab was booming during Year Two. The video collection of naturalistic data slowed to a comfortable pace and the collection of experimental data was all I could have asked for, and more. I should have been deliriously happy. I was certainly not unhappy, but I had withdrawn my emotional investment. I wanted to escape, and once again my personal direction was upstream to the actual course of events. But everything was going so well in my absence that I began to reconsider my conclusion that the kiddie lab had been a mistake. By the spring of 1975, while everyone else was reconciling themselves to the imminent demise of the lab, I began to wonder whether we could find money somewhere to continue it.

Space

"You can't park the boat by
me there, inside here."
Mitchell (Year Two)

On Tuesday afternoon, October 31, 1972, I was sitting in
Mike Cole's office. He was telling me about some data
he had collected in Harlem. It was shortly after my enroll-
ment as a graduate student in Developmental Psychology
and it occurred to me that I would understand it all a lot
better if I actually saw children being tested.

"Mike," I said, "if I took my tie off, could I go see your
operation?" Taking your tie off around Mike is like taking
your shoes off in Japan—it expresses respect.

"Great! Can you make it this Thursday?"

"Sure."

Mike called to his secretary. "Vera, see if you can get
those same reservations for Dr. Miller."

Reservations? Mike had been talking about data collected
in Mexico, not Harlem. That was how I got myself invited
to visit the Mayans in Quintana Roo, on the Yucatan Penin-
sula. Two days later I was in Merida, equipped with blue
jeans, Kaopectate, a pocket flashlight, a diary, and a copy of
Eve Clark's paper "On the Child's Acquisition of Antonyms
in Two Semantic Fields." Friday we drove from Merida to
Bacalar, in Quintana Roo; Saturday our two paid infor-
mants, Angel and Manuel, translated Eve Clark's "spatio-
temporal terms" into Yucatec Mayan; by Sunday morning I
was in the jungle vicariously testing monolingual Mayan
children through Angel. That is to say, Angel asked the
questions in Mayan and I took notes on what he said the
children said in response.

Eve Clark, a psycholinguist at Stanford University, had asked thirty white, English-speaking children in Palo Alto, California, to give the opposites to various dimensional and spatiotemporal terms. For example, if the experimenter said *up*, the child was supposed to say *down*; if the experimenter said *down*, the child was supposed to say *up*. Children younger than four were unable to understand the task; she tested children from 4;0 to 5;5. I decided it would be interesting to try to replicate this experiment with Mayan children, but I dropped the dimensional terms in order to simplify my initial venture in this kind of cross-cultural research. I regarded what I was doing in the spirit of a course assignment intended primarily to teach me something, not to add to the world's store of accumulated knowledge. At the same time, I thought that if something interesting turned up—some striking difference between English-speaking and Yucatec-speaking children, for example—I might become more seriously involved.

The general hypothesis Clark was exploring was that children become familiar with words before they understand exactly what they mean. A child might know, for example, that *up* is a member of the semantic field of spatiotemporal terms before he or she knew exactly what relation it expressed. Then, within any given semantic field, you might find some regular order for learning the terms, perhaps an order that would be predictable from a semantic analysis of their meanings. For example, *up/down* should be simpler, and learned earlier, than *over/under*, because *up/down* specifies only direction on the vertical axis, whereas *over/under* requires in addition a specification of the reference object. She reasoned that if a child knew the semantic field a word belonged to, his or her responses on the antonym test would be words in the same semantic field; that prediction was confirmed. And she reasoned that children would be able to give the correct response at an earlier age for semantically simple pairs than for semantically more complicated pairs; that prediction was also confirmed.

It seemed to be an important finding and the methodology was simple enough to use in the field. My first problem was to discover whether Yucatec Mayan has similar pairs of antonyms. I believe it does, but if a serious student of the language contradicted me, I would yield without a murmur. Three of us worked on the translation. I knew English and a smattering of high school Spanish. Angel knew English, Spanish, and Yucatec. Manuel knew Spanish and Yucatec. The first step was for me to explain to Angel the exact meaning of the English word, and to agree with him on a Spanish equivalent. The second step, in which I was an innocent bystander, was for Angel and Manuel to agree on the equivalent Mayan word. This process occupied a lazy Saturday afternoon in an open-air bar on the beach of the lake at Bacalar, where the accommodating proprietor could be consulted when Angel and Manuel disagreed. Although I was enormously impressed by the patience and intelligence of my two collaborators, I was left a little uneasy about the accuracy of our final list of Yucatec words.

In order to check on the translation, therefore, we decided to give the test first to some adults. This resulted in a couple of deletions from Clark's list before we called in a fourteen-year-old lad. Every subject we tested drew a blank on some of the words, but when Angel suggested the correct opposite they recognized it and agreed. By this very loose criterion of success, everybody "passed" our test. Then we tested a twelve-year-old boy. He made only a couple of errors, so we moved next to three eight-year-olds. They also managed it as well as their elders, so I called for still younger children.

At this point our friendly and helpful hosts were forced to disappoint me. Mayan children stay close to their mothers until about five or so, and even after that they are rather shy with strangers. We agreed that Angel would return without me and test some even younger children. Perhaps he did, but I never learned the results.

The venture was, therefore, inconclusive, to say the least. I think that Yucatec Mayan does have antonyms for spatio-temporal terms, just as English does, but Yucatec speakers had a lot of trouble thinking of them in a test situation that was perfectly comfortable for five-year-old American children. With this degree of uncertainty about the adult organization of lexical memory, I suspected that there might not be anything very substantial whose development in Mayan children I could hope to study. Fortunately, however, Mike has made me sufficiently aware of the pitfalls of drawing conclusions about what people cannot do on the basis of test procedures designed in a very different culture. It would take years really to understand what was going on; I spent less than a week. Perhaps a better way to say it is the other way round. In less than a week I was able to see that I would never understand the lexical competence of Mayan children; with American children it took me two years to learn that lesson.

There was one interesting finding, however. At the close of the antonym test, just out of curiosity and to provide a little antic relief from the tensions we had caused, I got Angel to throw in some questions about intrinsic parts. He would take a table, hat, bottle—whatever was convenient—and turn it upside down. Then he would ask our victim, in Mayan, to show him the top. All of the articles we tried that have intrinsic tops in English also have intrinsic tops in Mayan. When turned upside down, monolingual Mayan speakers pointed to the bottommost part (the intrinsic top) as "the top," and to the uppermost part (the intrinsic bottom) as "the bottom."

What I remember best was an elderly and dignified man who agreed to the test because he needed the five pesos we paid. When Angel turned a glass over and asked him to point to the top, he pointed to the intrinsic top. Then Angel pointed to the intrinsic bottom, which was uppermost, and asked whether that could be called the top. "Yes," the man replied, "but then it is not a glass." That summarized the theory of intrinsic sides in one simple sentence.

A year later, when the kiddie lab began operation, my curiosity about how children learn the intrinsic sides of common objects was still with me. Our children were too young to understand Eve Clark's opposites tests, but I thought it would be interesting to ask them questions like "Can you show me the top?" or "What is this side called?" Elsa Bartlett's doctoral thesis was a study of how young children use size words like *big* (the height of the object seems to be the important perceptual feature), so she was a natural ally in a study of sides. She read what Phil Johnson-Laird and I had written and agreed to tackle it.

During Year One, therefore, Madeleine Dobriner collected informal data on the children's understanding of deictic and intrinsic sides. Elsa and I discussed the theory, Elsa and Madeleine converted the theory into a variety of questions about specific objects, and Madeleine worked them into the playroom routine. The children seemed to know that *top, bottom, front,* and *back* were names for sides (we all agreed it was useless to test *right* and *left*), but they were not always correct in identifying which was which. Elsa had an idea that some children recognize intrinsic tops of objects if the top is a lid—if *top* is a name for a part, rather than a side, of a container. We wondered whether such specific items of information might represent their first steps toward a general rule. And she detected a tendency for the side with the most detailed features to be called the front—which led to success for things like toy chests of drawers, but to failure for toy stoves. They did best in identifying the sides of dolls and toy animals—with some giggling about the bottom of a doll (which was usually not the doll's feet).

I had assumed that the deictic system, which requires less information about particular objects, would be easier for children to learn. I even went so far as to speculate that they would learn the deictic system first and then treat objects with intrinsic sides as exceptions to the deictic rules. The data that Elsa brought me did not support this hypothesis about the order of development of side terminology, but it did not clearly refute it, either—the children were already launched into the learning process and I did not know how far along they were. But I was puzzled.

In the spring of 1974 I talked to Sue Carey about it. She made the cogent point that it was not really clear which system is simpler; the deictic system may be simpler for the speaker, but the intrinsic system may be simpler for the hearer. In addition, she had data that indicated two-year-olds already know a lot about intrinsic fronts. A student of hers at M.I.T., Susan Cohen, provided a tray of objects with intrinsic fronts—dolls, toy chairs, animals, cars, and the like—and put three or four of them, correctly oriented, in a "parade." When the two-year-olds were asked to continue the parade, they placed other objects in the line with correct orientation, front forward. Those children understood what the intrinsic fronts of many objects were before they knew the word *front*. The idea that the development of the deictic system could have preceded the acquisition of this knowledge of intrinsic fronts was absurd.

One lesson here is that analysis of adult patterns is a risky source of developmental hypotheses. The most obvious danger is teleological. With the end point clearly in view, a theorist may be tempted to think of it as a magnet drawing the developing child toward itself by some magical inversion of cause and effect. I did not stray quite that far from accepted scientific dogma—I recognized long ago that adult languages have the forms they have because children learn the way they do, and not vice versa. But I did fall afoul a less obvious danger, more logical than teleological. I assumed that the components of adult competence would appear as components of child development. At a gross level it is a good assumption, and when no better hypothesis is available it can be a useful first approximation at finer levels of analysis. The hunt does not get exciting, however, until this assumption fails. It failed when I assumed that the adult distinction between deictic and intrinsic labeling of sides would appear as a useful distinction in describing the first stages of a child's mastery of side terminology. At that point the real detective work began.

A second lesson is that in science you must expect to be scooped occasionally. You hope it won't happen, but you don't always get what you hope for. In January and February, 1974, Elsa had initiated some work in the playroom intended to explore our children's responses to sequences of objects. She designed a task that was very close to Susan Cohen's idea of using a parade to test for knowledge of intrinsic fronts. Elsa glued four objects in a row on a strip of cardboard, all with intrinsic fronts oriented in the same direction, and asked "Which is first?" The children pointed to one end of the row or the other—they picked the last object about as often as they picked the first, but they did identify one end of the series. Then she asked, "Which is last?" The children would then point to the object that was next to the one they had said was first. If she reversed the order of her questions, the same thing happened: the child pointed to an end object and then to the object next to it. One child was very explicit about it: he pointed to the leftmost object and said "He's first," then pointed to the adjacent object and said "He's last," and finally pointed to the third object in the row and said "And he's next." But these same children made no mistakes when asked which objects were at the front or the back of the line.

Elsa was well into this intriguing phenomenon, and other tests of serial order that she had invented, when she learned in March about Susan Cohen's parade experiments. Scoop number one. But since her ideas were not precisely the same, she decided she might as well continue. Then in October we came across a prepublication copy of a paper on fronts and backs by Michael Maratsos which, being already in press, scooped both Susan Cohen and Elsa. Scoop number two.

The history of science is so full of simultaneous, independent discoveries that the sociologist Robert Merton has made a special study of them. The number of instances of not-quite-simultaneous, independent discoveries is undoubtedly much greater. When you find yourself anywhere but first (or tied for first), the only way to dilute your disappointment is to do what Elsa did: tell yourself that you have so many other good ideas that you are bound to scoop the other workers next time. But it is still a disappointment, and one of the constant hazards of the scientific professions.

Although the simple question about fronts and backs that I asked Elsa to answer was answered first, independently and systematically, by others, her space program did not abort completely. She still had those puzzling observations about how children learn the meanings of *first* in line and *last* in line. In Year Two, therefore, she laid out a series of tests for Mary Jo to give in the red rug room, tests that explored not only the development of *first* and *last*, but also how they are related to *beginning* of the line and *end* of the line, and to *front* of the line and *back* of the line. Because her work with color terms took some unexpectedly exciting directions, Elsa had to postpone analyzing the results of these experiments on words denoting serial order. When she can get to it, however, the results should be of special interest. Four of those words—*first, last, beginning,* and *end*—are also used by adults to express temporal relations. And Joyce Weil collected detailed data on what these same children knew about time. Maybe we will learn something about the way spatial and temporal concepts intersect in development. There has been much speculation; a few facts might be very instructive.

So, the data collection is ended, but the analysis lingers on. It takes time to produce scientific results—a fact that I was too prone to forget in my impatience to see the kiddie lab come into being overnight. And that is a third lesson worth pointing out.

All in all, we learned a great deal from the work on spatial language, but not all of it was about spatial language.

Time

"When I was a baby I used
to be three."
Arthur (Year Two)

Man's most implacable enemy is his own invention. It's a shame that little children have to find out about it.

For sides or colors you can point to something. What do you point to for times? Clocks? No, clocks measure time, but they are not what they measure. The abstract nature of time has fascinated many great thinkers—at least one famous philosopher argued eloquently that Time is Unreal, whatever that means.

Psychologically, time has something to do with change. In a world where nothing ever changed, there would be no need for it. But when the state of the world changes from A to B, it is different from a change that takes it from B to A—time is the concept we invent in order to characterize that difference. It is a generalization of the concept of order, of succession. The appreciation of time is one of the fascinating faculties of the human mind—and perhaps of some animal minds as well, although man is the only animal who talks about it.

In industrial societies like ours, the concept of time has been refined and measured and standardized to what seem the limits of human ingenuity. It runs our lives and we think of it as a rare and precious commodity—most of us cannot understand cultures that treat time with indifference. Clocks and locks are the hallmarks of our civilization. Who else would build churches with steeples pointing to God, then put clocks on them? For all its abstractness, time is a very important concept.

The abstractness of time makes it a fascinating challenge for theories of language learning. It is all very well to argue that the word *red* is learned by associating red stimuli with the spoken form "red," but what is the stimulus to be associated with such spoken forms as "three years old," or "tomorrow," or "until"? Even if we could imagine aspects of stimulus situations to be associated with these words, what associations would lead us to relate them to one another in the way we do? I find it difficult to think about such questions without invoking a mentalistic explanation: the nature of the human mind is such that the *concept* of time is possible for us. We associate different words with different aspects of that concept, not with particular stimuli. I assume that the association is similar for other words as well, but for time words the conceptual component is theoretically indispensable.

When we undertake to study children's understanding of time, therefore, we are venturing into difficult territory. Is the concept innate? It is not clear what this question could mean. Perhaps it means, to borrow William James's phrases, that children are born with an impression of succession and do not have to learn how to integrate a succession of impressions. Perhaps it means they are born with a special sensitivity to changes. Perhaps it means they are born with the faculty of memory. I do not know. Whatever it means, children have the concept, at least in rudimentary form, at a very early age.

When we were selecting the lexical fields that would be appropriate to study with three-year-olds I thought that time words were too difficult. Without really thinking about it, I assumed that such abstract ideas could not appear until much later—until six or seven years, at least. It is true that many of our technical refinements of the concept—how to tell time from a clock, for example—are too difficult for three-year-olds. The following excerpt from a conversation during Year Two illustrates their confusion about longer periods of time:

Teacher: How about your daddy? Was your daddy ever little?

Girl age three: (Shakes head yes)
T: Yeah? When was he little?
G: Last week.
T: Last week he was little. How about your mommy?
G: She been little today.
T: Really? How old is she?
G: (Inaudible)
T: She's what? I didn't hear you. Say it again.
G: She's, uheee, three.
T: Three. And how old are you?
G: Three.
T: Are you the same age as your mommy?
G: (Shakes head yes)
T: How about your grandmother. How old is your grandmother?
G: She's five.
T: Umhm. How about your daddy?
G: Six.
T: Who's the oldest one?
G: My sister. I mean . . .
T: Your sister is the oldest?
G: No, she's the biggest. And I'm the oldest.
T: She's the biggest and you're the oldest?
G: (Shakes head yes)
T: Unhuh. I see.

This exchange is longer than most. Other children usually ended such questioning with "I don't know" before it had gone on so long. I believe the right view of this conversation is that the girl was playing a game with Madeleine. It is reasonably clear that she did not know the right answers. I think she recognized that her answers were odd, and she recognized that Madeleine thought they were odd, but as long as she could keep giving them she could hold Madeleine's attention. And she was able to keep giving them because, although she had not mastered the adult trick of mapping times into numbers, she did understand enough to make the right kind of conversational reply: time questions elicited time answers. Anyone who tried to use her bizarre answers as evidence that this girl understood nothing about the concept of time would be overlooking the very considerable progress that she had already made. She not only understood something about time, but she understood that times are expressed by numbers; exactly how this is done still had to be mastered, but at least she recognized the problem she faced.

The most primitive concept of time, perhaps, is that what is past is different from what is now. Bright children understand this difference before the age of three, and even have ways of expressing it. Early in Year One Joyce Weil clinched this point with a simple experiment. She asked Madeleine to introduce a cooking task into the playroom activities. At Madeleine's instructions, therefore, the children prepared batter and cooked pancakes. Madeleine's instructions were carefully worded in advance to include the time words *before* and *after:* "Put the milk in before you stir it," for example, or "Put the milk in after you add the flour." (She avoided such banalities as "Cook the pancake before you eat it" and such absurdities as "Cook the pancake after you eat it.") The children followed these instructions in the appropriate order far more often than would have been predicted by chance. Indeed, they did so well that Joyce feared that there would be no point in studying these words, that the learning phase was already over, but that was not the case. The children clearly had some understanding of *before* and *after,* but their mastery was far from perfect. I was particularly fond of this little exercise, because it strengthened my hope that meaningful experiments could be introduced naturally as part of the spontaneous activity in the playroom—that the experimental and naturalistic approaches could be integrated. It proved much more difficult, however, to get the children to utter "before" and "after" in their spontaneous speech.

Much later it occurred to me that one place the children expressed temporal concepts in their spontaneous speech was in their use of tense markers. Very early, usually at age two, children begin using the past tense forms of certain common irregular verbs: *went, saw, made, ran,* and so on. Somewhat later they catch on to the use of the dental flap, *-ed,* at the end of verbs, which results in correct past tense forms for verbs like *walked, looked, used, picked.* The use of the *-ed* suffix is overgeneralized, however, to the irregular verbs, resulting in such incorrect forms as *goed, seed, maked, runned.* This phenomenon is quite general and has been well documented; it provides one of the arguments for the view that children do not learn grammatical rules by imitation, because they do not hear the incorrect forms in adult speech and so have no model to imitate. They must create the incorrect forms themselves by applying a rule about *-ed* to all verbs. The same thing happens with the rule about adding *-s* to form plurals: *foots, tooths, mouses,* and the like could not result from imitation.

I had known about this kind of thing long before I became involved in studying children's time language, but I did not think of it in this context until late in the game. My block was an example of something that Karl Duncker taught psychologists to call functional fixedness. In my thinking, the function of such over-generalizations had become fixed on the argument about imitation; my fixation prevented me from recognizing their relevance to anything else—to the children's understanding of time, for example. One fringe benefit for being a psychologist is that when you catch yourself being dumb, you can usually find consolation by seeing it as an instance of some general principle that afflicts all mankind equally.

Once I saw the connection, my first assumption was that when young children start adding *-ed* to verbs, they must understand the concept of pastness; that is to say, they are expressing their recognition of the conceptual difference between *right now* and *before now.* The rule must be something like: adding *-ed* to a verb adds the concept of pastness to it. In order to use such a rule, you must be able to appreciate the concept that it presupposes.

If my assumption was correct, it was important. The question of which comes first, the word or the concept, has been hotly debated by students of cognitive development. I thought I had a clear case where the concept must come first, then *-ed* is recognized as a way to express it. In order to clarify my ideas, I decided to write them down. The tactic proved even more helpful this time than it usually is.

I immediately encountered complications. For example, according to the usual account of the over-generalization phenomenon, the *-ed* suffix is added to *all* verbs. That means, for example, that the suffix is added to *went* as well as to *go,* yielding both *wented* and *goed.* The trouble here, of course, is that *wented* is redundant: pastness is expressed twice. If the children understand pastness, why do they express it twice in the same word? Maybe redundancy does not bother them, or maybe they do it for emphasis. The question can be waved away, but I was still troubled by it. I decided that I needed some examples of these redundant formations. Perhaps I could explain them in some different way.

I turned, therefore, to our four authorized versions of the children's speech in Year One. It was not the kind of search that Peter Kranz's programs could do automatically, so I started reading through the transcripts myself, marking every occurrence of a past tense form in the children's speech. It was tedious work and maybe my attention flagged at times, but I found no occurrences of an irregular past tense form with *-ed* on it. (Later, one of Joyce's students repeated my search more carefully, with the same result.) Examples like *throwed, runned,* and *taked* were plentiful, but no *threwed, ranned,* or *tooked.* For example, at one point Don said, "He ate it. He drinked it all," where *ate* did not take *-ed,* but immediately afterward *drink* did.

I wrote Roger Brown about it. He referred me to his book, *A First Language,* where he had tabulated all occurrences of incorrect verb forms he had found in his protocols for the three children he had studied. My embarrassment at overlooking this table (I thought I knew his book backward and forward) was quickly forgotten in my pleasure with his data: there were forty-one occurrences of *-ed* being added to present tense forms of irregular verbs and only five occurrences with past tense forms. The children Roger studied were younger than ours, so a reasonable picture could be patched together. When children first start adding *-ed* they do sometimes over-generalize it to irregular past tense forms, but this redundancy is infrequent and, if my data are representative, shortly disappears.

This conclusion supported my hypothesis. If young children do not over-generalize *-ed* to past tense forms, they must have some basis for avoiding it. The obvious basis is that they understand that past tense forms already express the concept that *-ed* would add. Which is consonant with the assumption that they understand the concept of pastness. The hypothesis had passed its first test.

Another kind of complication was that *-ed* does not always express pastness. James P. Thorne impressed this fact on me during a brief visit from Edinburgh. Jimmy pointed to subjunctives: in the indicative, *I think he lived in Boston*, the *-ed* on *live* does express pastness, but in the subjunctive, *I wish he lived in Boston*, it does not. Fortunately, adults seldom use the subjunctive mood in talking to young children. Similarly, in passives like *Dinner is cooked by Mommy* the *-ed* on *cook* does not express pastness, but Roger Brown has data that indicate parents seldom use the passive voice in speaking to their children. Since subjunctives and passives are not part of the children's linguistic world, it is natural to suppose that such exceptions might escape them.

Other exceptions, however, are very much a part of the children's linguistic world. In sentences like *The toy is busted* (it is not clear whether this is an adjectival construction or a reduced passive), the *-ed* on *bust* does not express pastness. Young children use many such *-ed* forms—*It's gotta be hitched* was one example I found—where it would be strange to assume that the child meant *-ed* to express pastness. And there are even adjectives formed by adding *-ed* to nouns (*the bearded man, the blue-eyed baby*), where it is nonsense to ask about the tense of the noun.

Apparently, therefore, any rule that the children are using must be more complicated: something like, "Pastness can be expressed by adding *-ed*, but adding *-ed* does not always express pastness." After I thought about this complication for a while, I saw that it, too, was grist for my mill. In paraphrase, the rule says that the concept calls for *-ed*, but *-ed* does not necessarily express the concept. This means that the children must start with the concept and then notice that it can be expressed by *-ed*. If they tried to move in the opposite direction—notice -ed and then wonder what it expresses—there are so many exceptions that they would probably never develop a concept of pastness on the basis of the linguistic evidence available to them. The hypothesis had passed its second test.

A third kind of complication is still unresolved. If we ignore the progressive tenses, adults have three different ways to express pastness in the indicative mood: *It happened, It has happened, It had happened.* Children do not use *have* as an auxiliary verb in their earliest expressions of pastness; they have only the single form, *It happened,* to express all three. On the face of it, the children's concept of pastness would seem to be different from the adult's— simpler and less differentiated, perhaps. I prefer to think that the children at this stage can understand all three of the concepts of pastness that adults can express, but they have not yet learned how to express them. I think that when children use forms like *It happened* they are usually expressing the concept of pastness that adults would express by *It has happened,* and that it is the trick of shifting the reference time into the past that they have not yet mastered. But the arguments in support of my view are complicated and not totally convincing, so I will leave the question open here. Whether or not the children can differentiate conceptually among different kinds of pastness is not crucial to my hypothesis that they have *some* concept of pastness before they begin adding the -ed suffix to verbs. The hypothesis did not fail the third test. But I am still thinking about it.

When you pick up some linguistic phenomenon like this, you usually find a variety of complications dangling from it. You have to explore each of them in as much detail as you can (either that or rationalize not exploring them), and their exploration often raises still further complications. You are lucky when you can complete the maze and find your way back to your starting point. I will not claim to have settled all the questions raised by the children's use of -ed, but I have gone through enough of them to illustrate how this kind of argumentation goes.

In this case my starting point was the idea that children have a concept of pastness very early, long before they would be able to understand an explanation of this abstract idea. Since the addition of *-ed* is one of the first morphological rules that young children master, and since (if I am right) they have a concept of pastness before they start using *-ed*, the psychological origins of temporal awareness must be very primitive indeed. Joyce Weil was right; three years is not too early to undertake studies of children's time language.

In Year One, Joyce tried a more direct attack on the children's concept of time. The adult concept is conventionally represented as a line running from past (on the left) to future (on the right), with *now* as the point separating them. Does the time line characterize the children's concept as well? Joyce provided three sheets of differently colored papers arranged in a row, then took a toy animal and said, "*Today* the doggie is happy, so we'll put the doggie here," putting it on the middle sheet. Then she took another toy and said, "*Yesterday* the cat was sleeping—where should we put the cat?" Sometimes they put it on the same sheet with the dog, but if they put it on one of the other two, Joyce would take another toy and say, "*Tomorrow* we will see the horsie—where should we put the horsie?" She anticipated that children might find right-to-left as natural a representation of time as left-to-right, so the placement of the third toy was critical. If a child placed the three toys on separate sheets, and had them either in the order cat-dog-horse or horse-dog-cat, Joyce was prepared to take it as evidence that the task could be used to explore children's understanding of past and future points in time.

The pilot tests were sufficiently encouraging that Joyce introduced a series of more carefully designed versions of them during Year Two—varying the number of sheets, the order of the questions, and the time of the anchor (past or future, as well as present). The new results were inconclusive. They did not refute the possibility that children can think of spatial order as a representation of their concept of temporal order, because there was good reason to suspect that the children did not understand what they were being asked to do. But the results certainly did not support the idea, either. (Some children, perhaps expecting more questions about color, put everything on their favorite color!) The whole question of how children remember spatial versus temporal locations of events is a difficult one, however, that Joyce and Mark Altom attacked in a very different way during Year Two.

Before and After

"After breakfast we eat
cereal."
Mary (Year Two)

Harvey Sacks (one of the few sociologists whose writings I have studied carefully) wrote a graceful and important paper "On the Analysability of Stories by Children" in which he uncovered some of the concepts and techniques that are required in order to understand even the simplest uses of language. The text he took was the first two sentences from a story offered by a thirty-one-month-old girl: *The baby cried. The mommy picked it up.* Sacks made the following observations: (1) he understood this to mean that the mommy who picks up the baby is the mommy of that baby; (2) almost anybody who knows English will also understand this to mean that the mommy who picks up the baby is the mommy of that baby; (3) we understand that the event reported in the first sentence occurs before the event reported in the second sentence; (4) we understand that the event reported in the first sentence is the cause of the event reported in the second sentence; (5) all of the foregoing is understood without knowing what baby or what mommy is being talked about. The theoretical problem Sacks discussed is how we come to hear such sentences as we do, and what it means that all members of our language community can do it.

The baby cried. The mommy picked it up. This pair of sentences is recognizable as a possible description of something that could happen. In order to recognize some pattern of words as a "possible description" it is not necessary that you inspect what it describes. The hearer must understand what an observer might have seen—according to Sacks, a sequence of actions by an infant and a woman that the observer can relate in terms of a familiar cultural norm, maternal care. If the words and sentences can be interpreted as denoting such normal behavior, they will be taken as a possible description of it. Once the linguistic message is recognized as a possible description, the hearer can invoke the same social norm that an observer would; the hearer's assumptions about the baby's mother, the order of events, and the causal relation between events come, not from the words themselves, but from conventions associated with possible descriptions. If the story had begun: *The baby cried. The dog scratched its fleas,* there would be no norm to integrate the two sentences into a single description—it would be odd to imagine that the dog was scratching the baby's fleas. (Personally, I do not believe that social norms are the only devices we use to integrate events or sentences, but that would open a debate I have no desire to pursue.)

Sacks was eloquent about the importance of the fact that people are able to rely on the recognition of possible descriptions in communication. My interest in this example is more pedestrian. Note that the story did not begin, *The baby cried and the mother picked it up,* or *The baby cried, so the mother picked it up. And* and *so* are two of the earliest devices that children learn for making two sentences into one. I assume, therefore, that the author of this story was still too young to be using sentence connectives. The example is particularly apposite for Sacks's argument, since the usual signals an adult will give as to the relation between clauses—temporal sequence in the case of *and* or *and then,* cause-effect in the case of *so*—are missing and the information must be supplied by the hearer as a result of recognizing that the sentences are a possible description. If parents were unable to provide such supplementary information, communication between the generations would be even more difficult than it is.

It is remarkable that a child could have a mastery of the complicated social conventions for language use that Sacks described at an age when the various ways of conjoining sentences are still a mystery. Consider some of the alternative possibilities that a child must eventually master:

The baby cried and the mother picked it up.
First the baby cried, and then the mother picked it up.
When the baby cried, the mother picked it up.
The baby cried before the mother picked it up.
After the baby cried, the mother picked it up.
Since the baby cried, the mother picked it up.
The baby cried, so the mother picked it up.
Because the baby cried, the mother picked it up.

All of these are forward descriptions: the event described in the first clause is understood to occur before the event described in the second clause. We might, therefore, be tempted to think that it does not really matter how the sentences are conjoined. All of them are understood to describe the events in the same temporal order as the two sentences: *The baby cried. The mother picked it up.* The trouble with this view is that in language, as in dreams, effects often precede causes. The child must also learn that the following sentences convey the same temporal order:

The mother picked the baby up, but first it cried.
The mother picked the baby up when it cried.
Before the mother picked the baby up, it cried.
The mother picked the baby up after it cried.
The mother didn't pick the baby up until it cried.
The mother picked the baby up because it cried.

All of these are backward descriptions: the event described in the first clause is understood to occur *after* the event described in the second clause. They are *not* understood as describing the events in the same temporal order as the two sentences: *The mother picked the baby up. It cried.*

These are a few of the tricks that an adult can play with the order of his clauses. Tense provides still others. For example, we can give a backward description in two sentences by using *had: The mother picked the baby up. It had cried.* Or we can put the antecedent sentence in the future: *The mother will pick the baby up. It cried.* We can even do it

with the progressive aspect: *The mother picked the baby up.*
It was crying.

Sacks noted that starting to talk is a special matter for
small children, who have restricted rights for talking. If they
hope to be allowed to continue, they must make a beginning that warrants it. One way to do that is to announce
trouble relevant to the other person; an adult who began,
You're in bad trouble with Henry, would normally be expected to continue, and to command the listener's attention.
The young author uses a version of this strategy: *The baby*
cried announces trouble of the sort that adults are supposed
to be concerned about. It is, therefore, an appropriate
beginning for a story. None of the backward descriptions
share this feature; under the circumstances, they would not
be appropriate beginnings.

When we analyze a textual fragment in this way and
begin to see the variety of factors that must influence a
decision among the enormously rich set of alternatives that
language makes available, it can induce a kind of self-
consciousness about one's own speech. As long as we do
not try to explain these constructions, they flow ever so
sweetly from the tongue, but when we begin to think about
how much less is said than is understood, we begin to appreciate the true complexity of the communication system
the child is trying to master.

There is apparently something special about the story for-
mat, because children the age of this author do not normally
utter successive sentences related in this way. That is to
say, they may describe successive events in successive sentences, but there is seldom a causative relation between
them. In order to elicit spontaneous speech about temporally related events, we had to devise special activities for
the children.

We decided that causality was a bit beyond them (and
us), but temporal sequencing was not. Joyce Weil assumed
responsibility for studies of time language in Year One, and
in Year Two she really got going. Armed with a grant from
the National Institute of Education, she moved into the vacuum created by my discontinuation of the naturalistic re-

cording of Year One. With her talent for efficiency, she successfully hoarded her NIE money, allowing me to pick up more of the cost than I had anticipated, and not only launched a combined experimental-naturalistic study of longitudinal design, but enlisted her graduate students from Yeshiva University in a series of related, cross-sectional studies. She laid out a research plan in detail and programmed herself and her assistants to carry out the tasks one by one. I have already indicated something of the scope of her project in describing her administration of Year Two; here I would like to focus on some of her studies of temporal connectives.

Because Johnson-Laird and I had discussed connectives like *before* and *after* in a context of related words, Joyce decided to study sentences conjoined not only by *before* and *after,* but also by *and then, next, when, but first, while, until,* and so on. In a typical experiment the children's comprehension of these words would be explored by asking them to act out the events described in sentences that contained the connectives. For example, a child would hear a sentence like "Touch the doggie and then touch the doll," or "The doll fell down but first the doggie jumped over the fence," and would use toy animals and dolls to act out those events in the appropriate order.

In order to get some general sense of how difficult these various words are for children, two of Joyce's Yeshiva students conducted a cross-sectional study of ninety children between the ages of three and five-and-a-half, using test materials developed for the longitudinal study. They found clear evidence for learning during these years—the youngest children made many mistakes and the oldest made very few. They also found consistent differences in the difficulty of the connectives. The easiest sentences were those of the form *A and then B, A next B,* and *A before B;* the hardest were the backward sentences *B after A* and *Before B, A.* These differences were more or less as expected. The interesting result was for backward sentences of the form *B but first A.* Although some of the youngest children made mistakes on *but-first* sentences, from age three-and-a-half on it was one of the easiest (more than 95 per cent correct).

This result implies that the children's mistakes on the other backward sentences, *B after A* and *Before B, A,* cannot be attributed to any inability to reverse the order in which events are mentioned in the sentence. Moreover, many errors were made on forward sentences because children acted them out in backward order.

The hypothesis had been widely accepted that the youngest children, before they know what the connectives mean, always act out events in the order mentioned— a first-clause-first strategy—and so are always right on tests with forward sentences and always wrong with backward sentences. Because these cross-sectional data did not follow this pattern, we found them highly instructive.

Joyce wondered whether the youngest children could really remember such sentences long enough to act them out. She had Madeleine try a memory task in the playroom, but the children spontaneously helped each other; they could not remain silent when they knew the answer to another child's question. They had to be tested individually, but this, too, proved difficult. Joyce told Keith Stenning about the problem and, after some discussion, Keith suggested a way to solve it: put earphones on the children. It worked. When the children were asked to repeat to an adult what they had heard, they could understand the point of doing so—the adult had not been able to hear the voice and wanted to know what it said. With this innocent deception he was able to get children as young as two years to try to repeat sentences.

Joyce and Keith used this technique in a study that compared imitation and comprehension by the same children. Two more graduate students at Yeshiva were enlisted and they tested 72 children between three and six years of age. Because two tasks were involved in this cross-sectional study, the number of temporal connectives was reduced: *before, after, but first,* and *not until.*

Life is full of little surprises, however, and the life of a researcher has more than its share. This time the surprise was that the comprehension data from the second cross-sectional study did not replicate the comprehension data from the first. There was evidence for development with age, but all of the connectives seemed to develop at the same rate! It was bewildering, and reminded us all of how difficult it is to replicate studies conducted on small children.

The imitation data, however, provided some reassurance that these children really were mastering the connectives in the expected order, even though their comprehension data alone did not show it. The kinds of errors the children made were different for the different connectives. For the difficult connectives there was a greater tendency to omit the first event in the sentence because of memory failure, whereas memory failure played less of a role with the easy connectives. By analyzing these omissions, therefore, Joyce and Keith were able to show that the familiar order of difficulty could be obtained.

Thus, the overall pattern of development was reasonably clear, but many details were not. In particular, both of these studies raised doubts about the first-clause-first strategy. Joyce felt they provided equally strong evidence for a main-clause-first strategy: act out first the event mentioned in the main clause of the sentence. The complexity of the phenomena revealed by these studies, however, suggested that the learning process was neither simple nor uniform across children. Much remained to be explained.

Meanwhile, longitudinal observations in the red rug room continued. Joyce, taking a suggestion from Sue Carey, had introduced some test sentences with nonsense connectives: "Touch the doggie alshem touch the doll." If it is correct that young children will use a first-clause-first strategy when they do not understand a connective, meaningless words like *alshem* should produce a consistent pattern of responses. In fact, however, the responses were random: almost as many children acted them out in the reverse order as in the order mentioned, and several children performed both acts simultaneously. They did not respond to *A alshem B* the same way they responded to *A and B*. *Alshem* was not a member of this lexical field and the children's behavior did not look like their behavior with any other connective she tested.

With this much evidence that the first-clause-first strategy is more complicated than it looks, it is important to consider the longitudinal data. But first I should sketch the larger theoretical context of the first-clause-first hypothesis.

The theory was stated most explicitly by Eve Clark, on the basis of evidence from her own cross-sectional studies of *before* and *after*. According to her interpretation, children pass through three stages in their understanding of these connectives, stages that are characterized by the patterns of errors they make on comprehension tests. In Stage I the children do not understand either *before* or *after*; they respond to the test with a first-clause-first strategy, as if no connective had been used. In this stage, therefore, they make no errors on forward sentences (*A before B* and *After A, B*), but are consistently wrong on backward sentences (*Before B, A* and *B after A*). Stage II has two subdivisions. At Stage IIa they understand *before*; both forward and backward sentences with *before* are correct, but the first-clause-first strategy is still used with *after*. In this stage, therefore, they make no errors on *A before B, Before B, A,* or *After A, B,* but still make errors on *B after A.* At Stage IIb, all sentences with *before* are correct and all sentences with *after* are wrong, as if the children thought *before* and *after* were synonyms. Stage III is attained by children who realize that *after* is the antonym, not the synonym, of *before*. At this stage, therefore, no errors are observed.

Now, this is a strong hypothesis. Since there are four test sentences, either of which can be responded to correctly or incorrectly, there are $2 \times 2 \times 2 = 16$ possible patterns of errors. Eve Clark's hypothesis is that only four of these sixteen patterns will be observed in the data. Or, allowing for some variability in the children's behavior, other patterns of error may be observed, but these four should be the most common.

With Clark's hypothesis in mind, consider Weil's data. Tests of *before* and *after* were given four times during the school year; each of these four assessments can be looked at as a separate, cross-sectional study. When the data are analyzed in this manner, Clark's hypothesis is confirmed. The forward constructions were easier than the backward, and *before* was easier than *after*; Stage III (no mistakes) was attained only in the last assessment period. This confirmation is important, because it means that our data are probably representative of the kind of evidence on which Clark based her hypothesis.

In Joyce's study, however, it is also possible to look at the data longitudinally. That is to say, she could ask whether a child whose errors fitted Stage I on an early assessment later moved on to Stages II or III. When the same data were analyzed longitudinally, no evidence could be found that these were successive stages in the development of any individual child's understanding. On the average, the children were learning something about *before* and *after:* their correct responses increased from 53 per cent on the first assessment to 70 per cent on the fourth. But Clark's hypothesis was no help in predicting a particular child's development.

Where do these longitudinal results leave the first-clause-first hypothesis? It seems more and more of a puzzle. On the one hand, children evidently follow it in examples like *The baby cried, the mommy picked it up.* Moreover, the first connective most children learn is *and,* which serves a variety of semantic functions, at least one of which is to signal a forward order of events. And on comprehension tests many children do in fact show the predicted pattern of errors: all forward sentences right and all backward sentences wrong. But, on the other hand, the *alshem* experiment shows that a child who does not know the meaning of a connective will not automatically resort to a first-clause-first interpretation. Moreover, the fact that children can handle backward sentences with *but first* shows they are not incapable of reversing the order. And many of the error patterns on comprehension tests cannot be explained by any version of the first-clause-first hypothesis. Apparently, sometimes children follow a first-clause-first strategy and sometimes they do not. What conditions influence their decision is still an open question.

I have not told this story to discredit Eve Clark. She formulated a plausible hypothesis clearly enough that it could be tested—an admirable accomplishment—and, cross-sectionally, Joyce was able to replicate her results.

Rather, I have told the story to emphasize the value of what might be called minilongitudinal studies. Cross-sectional studies tell us what to expect on the average, but not what individual children do; they provide an envelope, but inside the envelope we may find many individual differences. The only way to determine whether individual minds follow the same course of development as the group mind is to track individual minds over a period of time—and that is precisely what minilongitudinal studies are designed to do.

I was gratified to learn that repeated measures on the same children could provide information unobtainable from cross-sectional studies. I had assumed that that would be the case; the assumption shaped my initial conception of the kiddie lab as a place to conduct longitudinal studies. Because Joyce's results with *before* and *after* (and also Elsa's on the order of learning color words) seemed to confirm my suspicion that cross-sectional data seldom tell the whole story, I may be exaggerating their importance. But it comforts me in moments of self doubt.

Color

"Blue. Where is blue?"
Roslyn

Historiography is an uncomfortable costume for my ideas. I have spent too many years searching for ahistorical principles—for propositions whose truth does not depend on the particularities of person, place, or time. Although I know that every event is unique, my imagination has been trained to ignore uniqueness, to value more the similarities that might support scientific generalizations. I would not change the bent of my mind even if I could, but it does handicap me as a narrator.

In telling this story, which aspires to be the history of a search for the ahistorical, the temptation is strong to subordinate the account of what happened to an explanation of what we were looking for. I want to give them equal billing, but I keep slipping into the more comfortable hypothetical mode. It probably has something to do with the way I file professional events in memory—in terms of the abstract ideas that were at issue at the time. Therefore, my memories are not arranged in temporal sequence, like laundry hung out on a chronological clothes line. Each substantive topic I think of brings to mind different events, which then I try to put in order. I should, perhaps, put all these different subsequences together in a single narrative. But that is not my way.

The lab had weekly meetings for lunch and shop talk. Coffee was provided and people brought whatever else they wanted from the University cafeteria. Usually somebody would summarize a piece of work accomplished or, more often, a piece of work projected. But sometimes we spent the hour planning the work in the kiddie lab. The incident that color brings to mind occurred at a lunch devoted to the assignment of topics to particular researchers. I infer that it must have been in October 1973, about the time we settled on space, time, and color as the three semantic fields we should follow. We quickly reached agreement that Elsa Bartlett would take responsibility for studying the children's spatial language and that Joyce Weil would do the same for their temporal language. Then I asked who wanted to study color words.

The ensuing silence lasted long enough for me to contemplate the possibility of taking responsibility for color myself. It did not seem a challenging task. Developmentally, color is not terribly important to children. Educationally, it has been worked to death. Psychologically, the perceptual and conceptual aspects are well understood. Linguistically, the lexical field is not complicated. The reason I pushed to include it was that the two semantic domains that have been studied most intensively are color and kinship. The logic of kinship relations is too advanced for three-year-olds, but color naming is within their grasp—intelligence tests indicate that children of average intelligence can name the primary colors by age four. On the assumption that the value of any new fact is augmented by the number of old facts it can be related to, I wanted our work to make contact with the considerable body of knowledge about color and color terminology that already existed. And I saw it as a relatively simple arena in which to grapple with the kinds of problems we would face in any study of semantic development, but that might be difficult to unravel for the language of space or time. I was determined that we should study color naming, even if it meant that I had to do it myself.

Before I could volunteer, however, Elsa raised her hand. She would do it. She told me later that she thought it would be a simple task, that she could collect the data and be done with it in two or three months. The months have since turned into years and, at this writing, Elsa is still interested in it.

Two kinds of tests had to be given. In a comprehension test, children are shown a set of colors and asked to point to the red one, or the green one, or the blue one, or whatever. If a child points correctly, it is evidence that the color term was comprehended. In a production test, children are shown a single color and asked to name it. If a child names it correctly, it is evidence that the color term can be correctly produced in the child's own speech. Comprehension is generally easier than production.

Both tests require sample colors that can be shown to the children. We invested in the Munsell Color Charts, and Elsa asked people around the lab to indicate the focal values for eleven color terms: the reddest red, the bluest blue, and so on, for red, blue, green, yellow, black, white, gray, brown, purple, orange, and pink. Then we bought colored papers matching the adults' consensus and used them to construct the test materials.

All this took time, and in the meanwhile it was a simple matter to explore the children's knowledge in a preliminary way by using various colored objects available in the playroom. Madeleine found that some of our children were already in control of the color terms, which was good for them but bad for us. Fortunately, some of them were just beginning.

Kevin was the best subject. When he told Madeleine that the color of a yellow bucket was round and that the color of a white plate was a plate, we knew that it was not going to be the cut-and-dried business we had anticipated. We were surprised; recognizing why we were surprised went a long way toward straightening out our ideas about how children learn color terms.

The simplest notion I can imagine of how children might learn their colors would go like this: you show them a color and, when you are sure they are looking at it, you say its name. Maybe you repeat the name in association with the color several times while you encourage the children to say it, too. When they do you give them some pleasant reward—smiles, approval, toys, candy, whatever is at your disposal. You repeat this sequence of color, name, and reward frequently until the association is firmly established. Then you select another color and repeat the procedure. This notion is a direct application of the familiar theory of learning that says that rewards (reinforcements, in the technical jargon) increase the probability of a rewarded response in the presence of a discriminative stimulus.

Since not all parents may take the time to provide this training in the self-conscious manner just described, one supposes that the stimulus-response-reinforcement sequence can occur spontaneously, without premeditation, in the course of parent-child interactions directed toward other goals. It is possible to question this supposition that a child's life naturally unfolds like a good textbook. But the theory is inherently plausible because it is biologically adaptive for organisms to repeat those responses that have led to favorable consequences in the past; organisms unable to do so would be at a serious evolutionary disadvantage.

What this application of the theory overlooks, however, is how children would learn the word *color*. I have trouble imagining how to teach it by the usual stimulus-response-reinforcement routine. Everything has some color; uttering "Color" whenever something is seen does not really count as evidence that a child understands what *color* means. Such training might even lead to confusion if, say, red must be called both *red* and *color*. How do you explain to young children that *color* is the superordinate term and *red* is the subordinate term?

There is more to be explained here than just the simple matter of attaching color terms to color stimuli. When Madeleine posed the question, "What color is this?" to Kevin, she presumed that he knew the word *color*. When Kevin said "Round" and "A plate," he was telling us that this presumption was incorrect. Kevin did not yet know that an appropriate answer to questions about color was some word like *red, green, yellow,* or *white.* Which set for us the problem of finding out what Kevin did or did not know about the more generic term, *color.*

Suppose children learn *color* like this: First they learn the names for all the individual colors and only after that do they learn that the general term for all those specific color names is *color.* However plausible such an account might seem to a logician, it is clearly wrong. Other children showed us that they knew what the color words are—they never answered a question about color with any words other than color terms—even though they could not consistently give the correct names to many color stimuli. Kevin himself passed into this more advanced state of understanding by the second time Madeleine tested him, perhaps because her questions called his attention to this neglected suburb of his vocabulary.

If children recognize words as color terms even when they do not know what colors they name, it would seem that quite a lot of learning must go on before—perhaps in preparation for—the eventual learning of name-color associations. It was this preliminary learning that we decided to focus on. Somehow a child learns that *red* is a color word and *round* is not a color word. That implies that he must be able to gather words into related groups: *red, green, yellow, blue* are related words in one group; *round, square, flat* are related words in another group; and so on. One set of words is appropriate in response to questions about color, another in response to questions about shape, and so on. But how do they know what the relation is when they do not know what these words denote? Is it simply a matter of rote memory for the different lexical units? Or do they have some general concept of the aspects that *color, shape,* and the like abstract from the total perception of an object? Or both? Or neither?

We opted for both. I like to think the children were in a state of ignorance about color terms somewhat comparable to my own ignorance about flower names. I know, for example, that *camellia, nasturtium, marigold,* and *gladiolus* are names of flowers, but I have little or no idea what they look like. In short, I have both a general concept of *flower* and a memorized list of subordinate terms that I could use in tests of comprehension or production, but I have never bothered to associate all the flower names I know to the blossoms they denote. Indeed, when it comes to secondary color terms, I am still in a very childlike state myself. But my subordinate terms, even though referentially vacuous, are associated with superordinate concepts, not mere superordinate words.

As the children's performances on successive tests piled up during Year One, Elsa and I began fashioning in our imaginations a sort of double-track theory, one track devoted to the linguistic knowledge that the children were acquiring and the other devoted to the conceptual knowledge that seemed to be required. On the linguistic track, we thought we could identify: (1) specific uses in particular contexts, like *red light* for a stop sign or *orange juice* for breakfast; (2) isolation of color terms from other words as a contrastive set; and (3) learning the referential value for each term. On the conceptual side we argued for: (1) abstraction of color from other aspects of visual experience; (2) recognition of the primary colors as special landmarks; and (3) location of other colors relative to the primary landmarks. The details, however, are still not entirely clear, because different parts are mastered at the same time, and because we could not make explicit the relation between the linguistic and conceptual accomplishments (which should be the heart of any truly explanatory theory). We suspect that different children learn differently, and therefore the correct generalizations are tantalizingly difficult to formulate.

Two other children gave us a different surprise. Although they never answered a question about color with anything but a color term, they used the same term for everything. What does it mean when, on a production test, a child calls everything blue? We knew it did not mean color blindness, for all of the children could sort papers correctly into piles of similar colors and all eventually learned to name them in the accepted fashion. It might mean that *blue* was the only color term the child knew, but we had independent evidence that that was not true. It might mean that the child had not yet mastered the simple rule that different-looking colors have different names, but that explanation seems rather implausible. I wonder whether it represents a strategy for learning what a color term means. If you are interested in the word *blue*, for example, call everything blue until you find out from adults when you are right and when you are wrong. We did not provide corrections in the production test, so the strategy did not work in that situation, but in normal situations it might be an efficient discovery procedure: indicate a succession of objects and ask for each, "Blue?"

Since the size of our sample was so small, we were uncertain how much trust to place in these observations. Months later Mike Cole dropped on my desk a translation of similar work by Z. M. Istomina published in Russia in 1958. She reported that 32 per cent of a large sample of Russian two-year-olds used a single color term to name all of the test stimuli. Perhaps this is simply the child's way of satisfying the tester's demands with a minimal exertion of cognitive effort, but, whatever the reason, our children were not peculiar in adopting it. It was a little disappointing to find that we had not made an original discovery, but it was encouraging to find that our observations were representative.

The results from Year One were of a preliminary nature. They taught Elsa what to expect and provided her with materials and procedures required for a more intensive study in Year Two. It was obvious that, if we were to add anything to the kind of results already obtained by Istomina and others, she should emphasize the longitudinal approach—repeated observations of the same children, instead of different children at different ages. But it is difficult to do a longitudinal study of many children on a limited budget. The problem challenged Elsa's ingenuity, and she solved it with the help of a nearby school. Her solution was to identify children who were just starting their first adventures in color naming and then, with their parents' permission, she tested them four times at six-week intervals between November 1975 and May 1976. In that way she managed to collect longitudinal data on 33 children between the ages of 2;4 and 4;0.

Elsa's way of doing a minilongitudinal study on color terms reflected a more general scheme for longitudinal studies of vocabulary growth. If we could enlist the cooperation of about thirty parents and teach them to recognize the first signs of an impending lexical development, they could call us in at just the critical time for the observations we wanted to make. We would not have to maintain a nursery school where we could look for the signs ourselves, and we would have a much larger population of children to observe. I have tried to sell Elsa's idea to various students of child language, but with little success. They comment that parents are untrustworthy reporters of their own children's accomplishments, that we do not really know what the signs of an impending lexical development are, or that longitudinal studies generally cost much more than they are worth. In spite of all that good advice, however, I remain optimistic, and so does Elsa. We talk about it occasionally and lament our inability to do any more than talk.

Before the 33 children were tested for comprehension and production of color terms, they were asked, "Do you know the names of any colors? What colors do you know?" The purpose was to see whether the word *color* would elicit color terms. It did: 32 of the 33 children gave at least one color term (most gave at least three); 30 gave only color terms in response; some gave color terms even though they did not name any colors correctly in the subsequent tests. Kevin's use of *round* in response to a question about color was not typical, even of the least knowledgeable children. Organizing words under the general term *color* is apparently the first thing they learn about this lexical field.

The repeated comprehension and production tests revealed a steady pattern of growth in color vocabulary; there was a strong correlation between the number of different color terms they used and the number of colors they could name correctly. Sometimes a child would seem to know a word, both in comprehension and production tests, and then on the next assessment a month later would not know it—some terms had to be learned two or three times. They had most difficulty with names for desaturated colors: achromatic *white, gray, black,* and dark, unsaturated *brown.* And there were consistent patterns in their mistakes, which were clearly not random guesses; they had definite ideas about what colors can be given the same name, even when the name given varied from one assessment to the next.

I was particularly gratified by Elsa's results on the order

in which different color words are learned, because they showed that repeated observations of the same children can provide information that cross-sectional studies cannot. Take one of the simplest hypotheses that has been proposed about the order in which color terms should be mastered. Red, green, yellow, blue, black, and white are psychological primaries with distinctive neurophysiological correlates. If these colors are salient, one might expect that their names would be learned first. And, indeed, when Elsa treated her data as if it were cross-sectional—simply pooled the tests for all the children and looked to see which terms were used and understood most accurately—the results seemed to support this hypothesis: of the seven terms most often used correctly, six were names of the psychological primaries (the intruder was *pink,* which was fifth on the list). But when she analyzed these same data longitudinally, this order was not characteristic of individual children. Of the fifteen who began in relative ignorance and acquired several color terms during the period of the study, only two mastered the six primaries before they mastered any other color terms. Individual orders of acquisition appear to be idiosyncratic, presumably depending on a child's interests and opportunities to learn. This finding pleased me because it suggested that minilongitudinal studies really are worth the extra effort they require—and that I was not completely wrong in my initial conception of the kiddie lab. On such slender threads is self-respect suspended.

Once Elsa was collecting data and we were debating alternative hypotheses about the learning process, she began inventing a variety of ways to explore the children's knowledge. For example, in order to test whether a child had an appropriate concept of color, Elsa would present toys that could be grouped either by color or function: a tan chair and a yellow chair, and a tan knife and a white fork, for instance. Then she would say (to a child who still did not know the referent for *red*), "Show me the red ones." Many children would pick the tan chair and the tan knife. That is to say, even those who could not name the color correctly recognized *red* as a color term and had a general notion of the referential domain at least adequate to enable them to group the objects on the basis of their chromatic similarity.

The comprehension and production tests are basic, of course, but much can also be learned by observing children's painting and coloring behavior—do they color grass green, water blue, and so on? Elsa showed children black-and-white photographs of familiar objects that have characteristic colors (bananas, oranges, and the like)—do they know the characteristic colors of such objects? She explored their memory for color by inserting a delay between showing them a color and asking them to pick it out of a set of alternative colors—do they remember better those colors for which they know the correct names? (Elsa's way of inserting the delay was to challenge the child to a race around the halls of the laboratory, where the length of the race determined the length of the delay; the price to her was to endure the feeble witticisms of the rest of the lab.) She constructed sequences of five color samples with two unattached samples to be inserted by the children—do they appreciate the standard sequence of hues? And she and Sue Carey devised a way to study the acquisition of a particular color term.

During Year One, in addition to creating the kiddie lab, supervising transcriptions, studying the children's spatial and color language, and trying to fathom what I expected from her, Elsa was spending her nights and weekends writing a Ph.D. thesis for Harvard. One of the readers of her thesis was Susan Carey, and during the winter and spring of 1974 Sue and Elsa had several conversations about the facility at Rockefeller. Elsa's enthusiasm infected Sue, which led directly to Sue's participation in our work during Year Two. Their collaboration added a new dimension to our study of color terms—in my opinion, an addition sufficiently important to deserve separate discussion.

In order to make its importance clear, however, I must first provide some general background about vocabulary growth.

About Vocabularies . . .

"One, two, blast off!"
Jeff

No doubt I am biased, but I think three-year-olds are very special. They are still babies on their third birthday; just beginning to explore, but always ready to retreat to a favored guardian; bold as lions one moment, shy as fawns the next. An old felt hat or a pair of high-heeled shoes can stir their imaginations and release their talent for imitation; we watch them and realize what babies they really are; we laugh at them and they laugh with us. And as soon as they have convinced us that they are wholly adorable, catastrophe strikes—a sudden fall, an unbearable frustration, a possessive jealousy—and they become just as wholly obnoxious; crying, whining, sniveling, using all the tricks that evoke comforting reassurances for babies.

As the year progresses, if all goes well, the fraction of the time they are babies decreases, and we begin to see what kind of persons we are dealing with. It is easy then to expect too much of them, to forget how much they still must learn. But I think we are right when we assume that the foundation for learning it has been laid, that the basis on which self-control and self-consciousness will develop is already irreversibly in place. I do not mean that they have not been learning before—far from it—but somewhere around their second birthday the nature of their learning begins to change, to become more open to and dependent on the world around them. By their third birthday the fruits of that worldly learning become apparent; not ripe, but clearly discernible. By their fourth birthday the cuddly infant is but a fading memory and they are well launched into the spontaneous apprenticeship we call the socialization process.

Psychologists disagree heatedly about the importance of language in these developments. Some seem to regard it as a mere tail on the developmental kite, an idiosyncratically human way to represent and express knowledge—knowledge that must first be achieved in nonlinguistic, prelinguistic ways. Others argue that it is language that gives children control over themselves and their minds, first through the speech of parents, later (becoming most obvious in three-year-olds) through their own speech to themselves—which eventually becomes covert, abbreviated, and is called thinking. I have no case to make for either view. For all I know, both may be equally right, or equally wrong, depending on what kind of learning one is interested in. It would, of course, add dignity to my own preoccupation with language if it should turn out that language plays a seminal role in all human development, but I have learned from children that dignity can be vastly overrated. It is enough to recognize that the transition from baby to child and the emergence of socially communicative language occur together. Whether one is cause and the other effect, and, if so, which is which, may be important questions, but I do not have the answers.

Up to about three years, diligent and attentive parents can keep a reasonable record of what words their child knows and how they are used. But then the process of vocabulary growth takes off, leaving the recording parent behind. The child begins using so many different words that it is no longer possible to recognize which are old and which are new; more indirect ways of estimating the size of vocabulary are required. Thus, for students of child language, three-year-olds offer a special challenge. They are on the threshold of a learning program that will accelerate through childhood and continue as long as they live. The three-year-old is just beginning a spectacular learning experience, the nature of which we know almost as little about as our grandparents knew about atomic power. Of course, psychologists who specialize in studying the processes of conditioning and learning have never been reluctant to propose theories about the mechanisms underlying vocabulary growth, but the very plausibility of those theories has made detailed observation of the child's spontaneous learning seem redundant. At best, however, these are theories about teaching. The staggering fact is that children acquire most of the vocabulary they will need as adults without being taught. If they were not able to learn far more than we know how to teach, they would never grow up to be like us.

Let me sketch the dimensions of this learning process, at least insofar as psychologists have been able to estimate them.

It is misleading to speak simply of "vocabulary learning," as if a person had one and only one vocabulary in which any particular word is either present or absent, known or unknown. There are many ways of knowing a word. At the very least, we must distinguish between a productive vocabulary of words a person actually uses, or is prepared to use, in his own speech and a recognition vocabulary of words he understands when others use them. People can understand a greater variety of words than they will use; their recognition vocabulary is larger than their productive vocabulary. For literate adults, the literary vocabulary is usually larger than the oral vocabulary, and within the literary vocabulary, again, understanding outstrips use: the reading vocabulary is larger than the writing vocabulary. When some claim is made about a person's vocabulary—about its size, for example—it is important to be clear which of these vocabularies is at issue. For example, if someone were to say that James Joyce's vocabulary was 29,899 words, he would presumably be making a claim about the number of different words Joyce used in *Ulysses.* Otherwise it would be impossible to reconcile the size of Joyce's vocabulary with that of an average college student, who has been said to know more than 150,000 words, as measured by a recognition test. Parental diaries show the development of a child's productive vocabulary; they must underestimate considerably the child's recognition vocabulary.

It is also misleading to speak simply of "words," as if it were obvious what a word is. Take an example. *Edit* is clearly an English word, but are *edits, edited,* and *editing* different words or simply inflectional variants of the same word? That is to say, does an English speaking person who knows *edit* know one word or four? In standard dictionaries, inflectional forms are all listed in a single lexical entry, and most vocabulary estimators have accepted that decision: *edit, edits, edited,* and *editing* are counted as one word. It would be more accurate, therefore, to say that what is being counted is not words, but lexical entries, or lexemes, as some linguists call them.

The answer is less obvious, however, for derivative and compound words. For example, is *edit* one word, *editor* a second word, and *editorial* a third? If *lap* is one word and *dog* is another, is *lapdog* a third word? Arguments can be made on both sides. In large dictionaries, derivative and compound forms are given separate lexical entries; if we are really counting lexemes, all these forms should be counted separately. But a psychologist feels that when a person who knows *edit, lap,* and *dog* learns *editor* or *lapdog,* he is not really learning as much as he did when he learned *edit, lap,* or *dog.* Since this argument seems unresolvable, careful workers usually give two estimates, one for the number of root words and another for the number of lexemes—root, derivative, and compound words counted separately. This is not as much trouble as it sounds; it simply means that you must treat the three kinds of words separately, as if you were giving three vocabulary tests in one, and weighted each kind with its own special sampling factor.

The problem is also complicated by the fact that most common words have more than one meaning. All of the studies I know count words, not meanings. For example, if a person knows *iron* only as a verb meaning to smoothe clothes by pressing with a heated flatiron he is given just as much credit as a person who knows that sense plus several others: a metal, a golf club, manacles. It would be a better estimate of how much a person knows if we could count meanings, but deciding what a meaning is poses even tougher problems than deciding what a word is. The conservative solution is to count words; the estimate would be much larger if we tried to count meanings.

All of which is probably more than any practical person wants to know about such matters. But it is still not enough to enable you to understand what psychologists are saying when they tell you the size of somebody's recognition vocabulary. You must also understand how the test is constructed.

Suppose you start with a large dictionary, one having, say, 500,000 lexical entries. Now suppose that you select 500 of those entries at random and use them to test Mary Doe's knowledge of the English lexicon. Then your sampling factor would be 1000. That is to say, for every item Mary recognized correctly, you can give her credit for knowing one thousand entries that you might have selected, but did not. If Mary recognizes 100 items correctly, your estimate of her recognition vocabulary would be 100,000 words.

Note how important it is to base your test on a very large dictionary, large enough to include all of the words that Mary knows. If you had started instead with a dictionary having 100,000 entries, each of your 500 test items would represent only 200 entries. In order to demonstrate that she could really recognize 100,000 different words, Mary would then have to answer every item on your test correctly. It is unlikely that she would be able to do that, unless by some odd chance the 100,000 entries in the smaller dictionary just happened to correspond exactly to the 100,000 words that Mary knows. But even if Mary were so lucky, her friend Richard Roe (who also knows 100,000 words according to the test based on the larger dictionary) would not be, because the 100,000 words he knows would surely differ to some extent from the 100,000 Mary knows. Thus it happens that the larger the dictionary on which a test is based, the larger the estimates of vocabulary size that you obtain. The reason is that most people will be able to recognize some words that are not in the smaller dictionary, and therefore the small-dictionary test does not give them full credit for all they know.

Is any dictionary large enough? Probably not. A child who grows up in a poor neighborhood must learn a lot of words not in our standard dictionaries, which are based on literary usage. He will not get full credit on a recognition test for all the words he really knows, and so may appear to be much farther behind a middle-class child of the same age than he really is. Since word recognition tests are an important component of most intelligence tests, he may even be told that he is much stupider than the middle-class child. And since the words that are in the standard dictionary do indeed seem to be words that teachers use in the classroom, his performance in school will probably validate the test result. With all this evidence piled up against him, the child may well conclude that he really is stupid and so give up any hope of academic success. That is one way "The System" keeps the poor in their place, a function that was socially acceptable as long as we needed large numbers of unskilled laborers, but in our present post-industrial society merely serves to fill the welfare roles and overpopulate the prisons. "The System" does not rely wholly on vocabulary scores to achieve this selective result, of course, but vocabulary is part of it and we should not lose sight of the larger social context for which our psychological investigations have significant implications.

We have still not said, however, how you are going to decide when Mary and Richard correctly recognize a word. One way is simply to ask them, "Do you recognize this word?" The dangers here are fairly obvious. Even if Mary and Richard are doing their level best to be honest, it is far easier to think you recognize an unfamiliar word than it is to forget you know a familiar word. A more objective test, therefore, is to provide alternative paraphrases of the word's meaning and to ask Mary and Richard to pick the right one. If you give, say, four alternatives, only one of which is correct, Mary and Richard could be right one-fourth of the time just by guessing. So you must subtract an appropriate guessing factor from the number they get correct in order to determine the number you should use in estimating the size of their vocabulary.

If you have followed this discussion, it is safe to entrust you with some actual numbers—you will not be tempted to find more accuracy or significance in them than is there, but will understand that these are simply the best estimates we have in our present understanding of these matters. The results I have most faith in were obtained by Mildred Templin and published in her monograph, *Certain Language Skills in Children*. According to her results (corrected for guessing), the median six-year-old child knows 13,000 words (7,800 basic or root words), the median seven-year-old knows 21,600 (12,400 roots), and the median eight-year-old knows 28,300 (17,600 roots).

In order to appreciate what these numbers mean, it helps to convert them into words learned per day. Between the ages of six and eight years, the median child learns $28,300 - 13,000 = 15,300$ words (or $17,600 - 7,800 = 9,800$ root words). Since there are 730 days in two years, this works out to be $15,300/730 = 21$ words a day (or $9,800/730 = 14.5$ root words a day). These numbers seem too large. Nobody self-consciously teaches a child 21 (or even 14.5) words every day. But all the other reliable data I have found give even larger estimates.

I think we must conclude, therefore, that children learn a lot more words than we teach them. Putting the results in terms of words per day does not mean that the learning process takes only one day—it may take only a moment, or it may extend over many months and many exposures. I assume that the process starts when a child first notices the word as something unfamiliar and persists at least until he recognizes it as familiar. At any particular time, therefore, a child must be learning several hundred different words that are in various states of incomplete mastery. But, on the average, he masters them at a rate of about 21 (or 14.5) words per day.

The dimensions of vocabulary growth that I have just sketched have been well known for many years. I myself reviewed them as long ago as 1951, in *Language and Communication*, but as long as I looked at them simply as normative data they made no particular impression on me. It was not until I began to wonder about the learning process itself that it occurred to me to translate them into words learned per day. That simple arithmetic exercise suddenly woke me up. Here was a fantastically broad and rapid learning process going on right in front of my eyes and I knew next to nothing about it! I had been taking it for granted.

When I decided to open my personal School of Developmental Psychology, therefore, one of the questions uppermost in my mind was how to study this kind of learning in detail. I had at least part of the answer. It was obvious that we would have to follow the same children over a period of time, so we needed something like the kiddie lab. And, since it seems impossible to follow *all* of the words children are learning at any particular time, I recognized that we would have to concentrate on limited groups of related words, groups of words that we could follow week after week. I felt we were in an ideal position to do that.

But then I was stuck. Madeleine and Elsa would test the children repeatedly, and would find they knew more words in the later tests than they had known in the earlier. We could tell pretty well what they knew at any time, and we puzzled over the pattern of growth from test to test. But the data told us little about how the growth occurred. We were looking at the result of the process, not at the process itself. The data added little to what we might have learned equally well from cross-sectional studies. Subsequently, Elsa discovered how to analyze the patterns in such data, but in Year One this situation contributed to my dissatisfaction with the work in the kiddie lab.

I remember thinking that we should try to teach them some new words, since then we could track the learning more closely—psychological journals contain literally thousands of teaching experiments. But that seemed to contradict our whole purpose, which was to spy on the children's spontaneous lexical learning. The project seemed to have reached a dead end.

. . . *And How They Grow*

"Hey, what's that called?"
Jeff

Susan Carey supplied the missing piece. It was the non-sense syllable, one of the most venerable tools in the kit of experimental psychology.

In the research for her doctoral dissertation, Sue had puzzled over the fact that a young child who is presented with a pitcher and a half-filled glass of juice, and who is told to "Make it so there is less in the glass," will usually pour more in the glass. She refused to believe that such children think *less* means *more;* when presented with a glass and pitcher and asked to do something, pouring from the pitcher into the glass is the most natural response if you do not really understand what you have been asked to do. Perhaps a child told to "Make it so there is tiv in the glass" would also pour from the pitcher into the glass. She tried it. Children at the appropriate stage of ignorance responded to *tiv* the same way they responded to *more* and *less.* Clearly they could not have learned anywhere that *tiv* means *more,* so why should we think they had learned that *less* means *more?*

By chance, a research assistant in a follow-up interview several weeks later happened to ask the children what *tiv* meant. Some of the children—those who were just beginning to learn *more* and *less*—thought *tiv* meant *more.* Children who had already mastered *more* and *less,* and children who had not yet begun to learn these words, did not know what *tiv* might mean, but children who were in the midst of getting these words straightened out remembered *tiv* weeks after a single exposure to it. Sue had the wit to recognize that this was a remarkable feat of memory. When, in the spring of 1974, she talked to me about what she hoped to do in the kiddie lab, she told me about this serendipitous observation and said that she wanted to follow it up. Our research facility offered an ideal situation in which to do so.

I know that I was impressed and enthusiastic, but I believe that I did not initially appreciate the implications of what she was telling me. That is to say, I did not immediately recognize that she was offering me the missing piece required to complete the program in which I had invested so much time, thought, and money. It was simply one of several ideas she was interested in, and I saw it then as just another item on our research agenda for the following year. I think I could not really have understood it, because I am reasonably certain that she put this final piece in my hands *before* I blew up and decided to close the kiddie lab. If I had appreciated it, I would probably have felt very differently about what we were doing. In self-defense, I should say that it was not then an established fact—you do not normally alter long term plans on the basis of a chance, and possibly accidental, observation. But that is a weak excuse. I should have been more perceptive.

Sue shared my view of young children as sucking up words like little vacuum cleaners. Her idea was to drop a nonsense syllable into their intake and follow what happened to it. She did not want to teach them the word, in any ordinary sense of "teach," but simply to insert it into conversation in as natural a way as possible, much as any other unfamiliar word might occur. The advantage of using a nonsense syllable was that we could be sure it was unfamiliar and that the children would not encounter it outside the playroom—we would have a complete record of all their experience with it.

I have a personal favoritism for studying verbs—too much psychological research in this area has proceeded as if "word" and "noun" were synonymous—so I tried to persuade Sue to find some gap in the verb lexicon, some simple verbal concept for which English does not happen to have an explicit verb, and to take that as the meaning of the nonsense syllable. I still think it was a good idea, but fortunately Sue recognized that something simpler would be required for a pioneer venture in this kind of research. After she had talked to Elsa Bartlett about it, they sensibly decided to exploit all that Elsa had already learned about how children master color terms.

They chose the color that adults would call olive, which is a reasonably distinctive color for which none of the children had learned any distinctive name. Their plan to use a nonsense syllable as the name ran into opposition, however; one of the mothers objected to having her child taught nonsense. After some negotiation, a compromise was reached. Like most compromises, neither party was completely satisfied, but it did enable Sue and Elsa to proceed with the study. The agreement was that olive should be called *chromium*, which is an English word that is sometimes used in secondary color terminologies, and a word that we were reasonably sure none of the children knew.

The important decision was how to insert the word unostentatiously into the child's linguistic world. It would clearly not do to point to a sample of the color olive and say, "This color is called chromium"; that was the kind of self-conscious teaching we hoped to avoid. Instead, one cup and one tray in the classroom were painted olive. There was one identical cup (red) and one identical tray (blue). In a natural context—while preparing for snack time, for example—Madeliene asked each child individually and apart from the other children to "Bring me the chromium cup; not the red one, the chromium one," or to "Bring me the chromium tray; not the blue one, the chromium one." Initially, only one such request was addressed to each child.

This particular method of introducing the word was chosen because it did not involve calling the child's attention to the fact that this was a new word. Sue wanted a strong test of the child's efficiency as a word learner. In order to carry out the task correctly the child did not need to focus on the word *chromium* at all; the phrase *not the red one* or *not the blue one* was sufficient to enable the child to comply with the request. The method worked smoothly. None of the children had any trouble picking out the correct cup or tray.

Most of them asked for some confirmation: "You mean this one?" And four of the fourteen children studied repeated spontaneously an approximation to "chromium." That is to say, most of the children overtly demonstrated that they had registered the occurrence of a new word, even though they did not have to know that word in order to carry out the request.

In order to assess the effect of this experience, it was necessary to compare the children's behavior before the event with their behavior following the event. Before they had heard olive called chromium, most of the children called it *green* and a few called it *brown*. One week after their single exposure to *chromium*, each child was given a comprehension test, in the course of which the child was asked to point to various color samples as they were named. When they were asked to point to the chromium chip, six children picked the olive one—which is suggestive but not conclusive, because they may have simply matched the odd color to the odd name—and three children identified the green chip as *chromium*, as if *green* and *chromium* were names for the same color. Thus, almost two-thirds of the children may have learned something about the word *chromium*, but the evidence was not yet conclusive.

No more references to chromium occurred until a production test six weeks after the initial exposure. At that time each child was asked to name a set of color samples that included olive. Eight of the fourteen children gave a different response to olive from the response they have given before exposure to *chromium*. Two said they did not know what it was called; they had learned that olive has a different name, but they could not remember what it was. Six others used another term for it—*gray, blue, brown*—but not the term they had used before the *chromium* experience; they remembered that olive is not called *green*, but they came up with alternative color terms whose reference they were not yet sure of. This evidence that the exposure to *chromium* had left its mark was more convincing.

Needless to say, these results were pretty exciting. Eight of the fourteen children began to restructure their terminology for the color domain (they learned that olive is not green) on the basis of a single experience. We had learned to expect some fluctuation in naming from one test to the next, but to have so many children change their response to the same color could hardly have been a coincidence. Unless Sue and Elsa were extremely unlucky victims of bad sampling, they did seem to have found a handle on a very rapid, efficient, and important kind of learning—the kind of rapid lexical learning that all the normative data call for.

It was, of course, only a pilot study suggesting that a method was available for more systematic investigations to follow. A number of important control conditions needed to be run. And they needed to study many more children, to introduce a variety of lexical items, to explore alternative ways of presenting the novel word, to develop systematic procedures for assessing the effects of single and multiple exposures. But all the pieces were in place. Now at last we knew how to attack the problem.

Following the initial exposure to *chromium* and the assessment of its effects, a few more exposures were provided and assessed in the same way. The results were summarized briefly in a paper that Sue Carey presented at M.I.T. in March 1976 and from which I will quote: "Two different routes to full acquisition were identified. Some children adopted a false hypothesis about the structure of the lexicon—that *chromium* was a synonym of *green*. In production, they usually called both olive and green *green*, but sometimes called focal green *chromium*. In comprehension, they often picked green when asked to choose the chromium chip. For these children, working out the correct lexical relationship between *chromium* and *green* was an extended process, not completed after fifteen weeks of testing. One child called green *light chromium*. The other group, in contrast, from the beginning knew olive needed its own name, and in production said they could not remember the name, or chose some color name with no stable referent. These children always picked olive in comprehension of *chromium*. Children who adopted this odd-color-odd-name strategy also did not all achieve full mastery by the end of testing."

After the children had been exposed to *chromium* several

times, some of them began to use it spontaneously in their own speech. Since they had not all settled on exactly the same meaning for it, the result was sometimes confusing. The following conversation was recorded late in March, while the children were weaving colored papers and yarns through small baskets intended to hold Easter eggs. The colors they were working with were fuschia, light green, and dark green.

> *Albert:* I want chromium, ah, a green, a green, I mean chromium and that red.
>
> *David:* They're pinks, not red.
>
> *Madeleine:* Ellen, which one do you want?
>
> *Ellen (indicating dark green):* The dark one.
>
> *Albert:* No! That's chromium.
>
> *Ann (yelling):* I want redpink, REDPINK, *REDPINK!*
>
> *David (picking up fuschia-colored yarn):* Chromium?
>
> *Albert (taking fuschia from David and giving him dark green):* No. Chromium is a green one.
>
> *Lynne:* I want a green one.
>
> *Madeleine (offering both light and dark green):* Which one?
>
> *Lynne:* Doesn't matter, but not red.
>
> *Ellen (picking up a dark green strip of paper):* Is this the chromium tray?
>
> *Madeleine:* What do you mean?
>
> *Ellen:* It doesn't look the same.
>
> *Madeleine:* The same as what?
>
> *(Ellen looks confused and does not respond.)*

Ellen was right, of course. The dark green did not look the same as the olive green that had been called chromium. Ellen was one of the children who adopted the odd-color-odd-name strategy; Albert was one who adopted the synonym strategy. But in both cases it is clear that *chromium* had been accepted into the lexical domain of color words, even though its exact range of reference was still under dispute.

Learning a new word under (nearly) normal circumstances thus has two stages: first, a quick pickup of the unfamiliar item and a general assignment of it to a particular semantic domain; second, an extended period in which the details of its meaning, relative to the meanings of other words in that domain, are slowly worked out. What is immediately appreciated and what is slowly uncovered will no doubt depend on the particular semantic domain—that is a topic for further study. But the first stage in which a new word is noticed and some first guess made about its meaning would seem to be a special, if not unique, kind of learning.

The results of the *chromium* study came in gradually; not until the spring of 1975, near the end of Year Two, were Sue and Elsa confident that they had found a practical method to study the spontaneous acquisition of new words by young children. In retrospect, it seems like a reasonably obvious way to go about it. When they write it up for publication they will probably omit all the trouble we had in thinking of it. Sue Carey and Elsa Bartlett are good friends of mine; I can count on them not to crow in public over the fact that they solved a problem that I could not. But that is how science in general edges forward. One of the best ways to decide that you have had a good idea is to recall how confused you were before and how obvious everything seems after you had it.

By the spring of 1975, therefore, we finally knew how to use the kiddie lab to study the growth of vocabulary. A major program to follow up this breakthrough was clearly needed. That was when the money from The Grant Foundation ran out and the lab was closed.

On Closing Schools . . .

"No, don't knock down my
building."
Jeff

If I seem to have devoted too much attention to problems
of funding the research I wanted to do, then I have represented accurately the salience of such problems in the
thinking of anyone who hopes to do research. The only person I know who claimed to have beaten the system was the
brilliant Hungarian physicist, Leo Szilard, who applied for
money to support research he had already done and spent it
to do the research he would apply for support of next. He
said this strategy worked beautifully for many years—until
a review panel decided that the research he proposed to do
(which he had already done) was impossible.

During the winter of 1973–74 Mike Cole and I drew up a
proposal that we mailed off to the Public Health Service for
consideration by the National Institutes of Health, where it
was eventually referred to the National Institute of Child
Health and Human Development. At that time the work in
the kiddie lab was still heavily naturalistic and my part of
the application was essentially a description of what we had
been doing, as if we contemplated an endless accumulation
of video-tapes and transcriptions. I would have preferred to
ask support for an experimental program, but the experiments I wanted had not yet materialized. As I said earlier,
in April 1974, when I decided not to continue the program,
Mike agreed to withdraw the application and Carl Pfaffmann wrote a letter to that effect to the NICHD. It sounds
simple enough. We had changed our minds.

Shortly thereafter we were informed that a site visit had

already been arranged and that the review panel would like to continue with their visit as planned. We had never heard of such a thing. How did they propose to review a nonapplication? Carl, Mike, and I shook our heads, shared an acquiescent shrug, and told them to come ahead—as much out of curiosity as hope. After all, Mike still wanted to do the work proposed in his part of the application, which included studies proposed by other members of his laboratory. Perhaps they would agree to an on-the-spot revision of the application that simply deleted my half of the budget. I, always a dreamer, began to think that maybe I could outline an alternative research program that I considered worthy of the funds I had requested. Hope springs eternal.

On the appointed day early in May the site visiting team arrived and we assembled in a seminar room in the Tower Building. Since most of the visitors had been chosen because of their experience in the kind of research I had proposed, they were curious to know what my group was doing and why I had withdrawn. Consequently, the morning was spent talking about my problems. I tried to introduce a hastily prepared, alternative plan for using the money I had requested, but they brusquely ignored it— they had not come to Rockefeller to buy a pig in a poke. They preferred to press their criticisms of the proposal as written, which was safe ground—I could not disagree with them. They made it clear that if I had not withdrawn the proposal, they would not have endorsed it; they seemed a little put out that I had beaten them to it. They wanted a chance to say that a facility of the type we had created was not needed; that if it was needed, Rockefeller University was not the place for it; and that, if it was at Rockefeller, they were not impressed by the competence of the people who were running it. After I had taken as much of this as I could bear, we took them to the fourth floor and showed them the facility. By that time their minds were closed. I found myself describing the video and audio equipment to my Rockefeller colleagues while our visitors chatted with each other. Finally one of them interrupted her conversation to ask impatiently why they were wasting so much time on the part of the proposal that had been withdrawn. With that, they went to lunch.

In the afternoon it was Mike's turn. Mike described a set of related research questions and, being aware of reviewers' hunger for specifics, sketched experimental designs that might be used to answer them; his colleague, A. J. Franklin, outlined several studies of memory that he wanted to do. This opened the door for lectures on experimental design and a study-by-study critique. Like sharks who had smelled blood, they attacked every vulnerable detail. Since none of the visitors had done comparative studies of the type Mike was proposing, most of the criticisms were pointless. Mike did not appreciate being treated like a backward graduate student and was embarrassed that A. J. was caught in the crossfire. He had trouble controlling his temper, and I felt miserable that I had set him up for it.

Our visitors concluded that research funds were too limited to justify giving them to anybody who did not have a clearly defined plan that included an exact account of what would be discovered and what use it would be. My facility was a needless extravagance; Mike's experiments were not well conceived. Once it became clear that they had no intention of revising the proposal to cover only Mike's part of the work, we left them to take their vote. Our nonapplication was rejected.

I estimated that I needed at least $50,000 a year just to operate the facility—to provide a teacher, someone to coordinate the research, a modest crew to transcribe and edit selected video tapes, a part-time computer specialist to process transcriptions, and such miscellaneous necessities as supplies, equipment maintenance, computer rental, and secretarial services. With that core support in hand, I thought we could submit a number of smaller, targeted applications for specific studies, proposals definite, modest, and relevant enough to appeal to cost-conscious review panels. Without the core support, however, the cost of running the facility would have to be padded into the targeted applications, which would make them less attractive and would leave the facility vulnerable to fluctuations in our sales appeal. It was too risky. Without core support of the kind The Grant Foundation was providing (and which terminated 30 June 1975), I saw no alternative but to proceed with my plan to close the kiddie lab.

Thus, the flurry created by the unexpected site visit left things about where they had been. But not quite. I had learned something. At first I was angry, but once I could overcome my resentment at the nasty way they said it, I recognized that our visitors were telling me something. In my translation, it went like this. American society is relatively generous in providing facilities where children of all ages can be cared for and educated. Instead of going to the considerable expense of duplicating such arrangements in the rather unnatural environment of a laboratory, why not exploit the facilities already avilable? Mike had already established working agreements with numerous New York schools and day-care centers. It would be a simple matter to take advantage of them.

The advantages of the kiddie lab, of course, were its convenience (the children came to us, not vice versa), the availability of video equipment (which could be carried off campus, but would probably be disruptive), and the possibility of longitudinal studies (which are difficult to conduct in most schools, given the transient nature of New York residents). Were these advantages worth $50,000 a year? Convenience is important but hard to justify, since it translates so easily into laziness. I had already decided that the video equipment was an extravagance, better reserved, like cavalry charges, for crucial moments. And Elsa Bartlett had proposed an interesting way of recruiting parents to bring us children on the verge of learning some new semantic field so we could follow, in minilongitudinal studies, particular lexical developments we were interested in. I could not convince myself that there was anything we wanted to do that could not be done without the expensive facility on the fourth floor. If only we wanted earnestly enough to do it.

At this point in my thinking I had to examine my own motivation. I quickly decided that I did not personally want to visit day-care centers and talk to three-year-olds. Even if the idea had appealed to me, I was sure they would not have been equally eager to talk to me. So the question became whether I wanted people in my lab who would visit day-care centers and talk to three-year-olds. Here my feelings were more positive, but once again my thoughts hinged on financial considerations. These people in my lab, how would they be paid? Without an adequate budget to hire them, I had been relying on adjunct appointments. Why would it be any easier to visit day-care centers from an office at Rockefeller than from an office anywhere else? Without an operating research facility, what advantages could I use to entice them? I could think of a few fringe benefits, but the prospect did not appeal to me.

The longer these debates raged in my head, the more reconciled I became not only to closing the kiddie lab, but to closing my personal postgraduate School of Developmental Psychology. I decided to adopt a passive, opportunistic attitude. I would not try to persuade people to join me in the study of child language, but if they wanted to, I would accept them. And I would not try to raise money to continue the kiddie lab when the Grant grant ran out, but if money unexpectedly turned up, I would accept it gratefully. With my personal ardor to learn about child development in abatement, I would let events take their course and make my decisions for me. I was reasonably confident where that attitude would lead me, but I would not rule out the possibility of some unexpected miracle.

My disappointment at the fate of our nonapplication was alleviated somewhat by subsequent events. As the saying goes, you win a few and you lose a few. I mentioned earlier that in April 1973 Bill Estes had submitted a proposal to the National Institute of General Medical Sciences for a continuation of a program grant that would have supported Bill, Mike, and me. That proposal had been enthusiastically reviewed, but appropriations had been impounded and the grant could not be funded. By the summer of 1974, however, the Presidential policy of impounding appropriated moneys had been overturned in the courts and NIGMS was able to fund the application, at least in part. A reduced budget covering work by Mike and me was submitted and we received a grant to run for three years, from 1 November

1974 to 31 October 1977, about $40,000 a year of which could be used to support the work in my lab. This fortunate development insured that I would stay in business, at least at a modest level of activity, and did nothing to shake my fragile faith in miracles.

As Year Two unfolded and the experiments I had despaired of began to appear, my lost confidence in the wisdom of my original plan for the kiddie lab began to return. I could not quite bring myself to submit another proposal to NICHD and take that kind of drubbing again, but I began scanning the horizon for possible miracles. The Grant Foundation was out, of course; they made that clear when they rescued us in 1973. But there were other foundations. I debated with myself whether to approach them, but my conflicting feelings about the kiddie lab and my preoccupation with finishing The Book with Johnson-Laird prevented me from going beyond covert debate. Then a foundation approached me.

During the winter of 1974–1975 the Rockefeller campus was visited by representatives of the Lilly Foundation, who claimed to be searching for programs worthy of their support. No university treats such overtures lightly; an elaborate tour of potential beneficiaries was laid on. Among the laboratories on their agenda were Mike's and mine; we played show-and-tell with them in our most ingratiating manner. I remember well their special sympathy with my complaint about the difficulty of finding core money to support a research facility in which a variety of specific (and more easily funded) peripheral projects could be conducted.

It was a pleasant visit. Mike and I were even more pleased when we learned that our work was of special interest to them. With their encouragement, therefore, Rodney Nichols, a vice-president of the University, put an elegant description of our work together with a generous budget (the size of the request was agreed to by the representatives of the Lilly Foundation) and sent it off with high hopes. I really expected something to come of it. I began to revive my plans for the kiddie lab—not just think about them, but think them, as if they might come true.

It was not until April 1975 that we heard from the pleasant gentlemen who had visited and encouraged us. They had been overruled by Mr. Lilly himself. Mr. Lilly wanted his Foundation to support practical projects that would have a more immediate and tangible social impact. Maybe in some future year the Foundation would be able to support the sciences that support the practical applications, but this year Mr. Lilly had a different idea. They were very sorry.

So was I. Not so much sorry that my miracle had failed as sorry that I had allowed myself to start dreaming again. Waking up is so painful. I fall in love with certain plans; waking from them is like the loss of a dear friend. Of course, I should have known better. Mr. Lilly was no different from other potential donors I had talked to: an initial expression of interest when they hear we are working with children, followed by chill silence when they grasp how remote our work is from newspaper headlines. I even sympathize with them. They want to solve society's problems right now, for unless we do something now, we may not survive to enjoy the eventual benefits of basic research. But I was disappointed anyhow.

It was about this time that Jerry Bruner visited. I told him about my problems in raising core money to support the kiddie lab and he listened with the patience of an old friend. At dinner that night he commented (not to me, but in my hearing), "George thought he could solve all the problems of developmental psychology by taking pictures of them." Jerry was trying to be witty, not offensive, but there is ambivalence in even the closest relationships. I thought about the remark for a long time. It presupposed my innocence, asserted our accumulation of a mountain of video-tape, and implied a fiasco. The truth in it was flawed by ignoring the work of Year Two, but any answer I might have offered would have taken a long time, sounded very defensive, and come out about where Jerry's rapier wit went in. We did take a lot more pictures than anybody needed.

Year Two wound down finally to 30 June 1975 and the kiddie lab expired along with the support from The Grant Foundation. There was a final frantic burst of effort to complete the transcribing, and Madeleine stayed on a while to complete her editing. But the playroom was closed, the children were gone, the adventure was over. The University submitted an accounting of our expenditures to The Grant Foundation and I wrote a brief final report for them summarizing what we had done.

But I was not satisfied. One undischarged obligation was to make the tapes and transcriptions we had accumulated available to responsible research workers. That would be expensive, however, and I was not sure how we could do it. Another obligation was to document the circumstances under which our data were collected, so that people who did use them would not have to repeat all that in every article they wrote. The whole group agreed that some such account should be written and published; Madeleine Dobriner, Peter Kranz, and I agreed to do it. Madeleine and Peter dutifully prepared detailed descriptions of their work, which sat on my desk unread for many weeks. My feelings were complicated. I remembered Jerry Bruner's comment. I remembered all the experimental work that was done in Year Two. I contemplated the prospect that the only part of our work I would publish under my own name was a description of the naturalistic phase that caused me so much anguish. I rationalized and procrastinated. I did not want to do it, but I felt obligated to.

Finally, in April 1976 (why do I make so many decisions in April?) I decided to tell the whole story, as I saw it, warts and all. Well, not the *whole* story, perhaps, but enough to give a balanced picture of what we were up to. It has turned out to be a rather unusual final report.

Still Other Personal Matters

"I build my own thing, I think.

Don

Le génie n'est qu'une grande application à la patience. According to my desk dictionary, *patience* is any admirable endurance of a trying situation or person, usually through a passiveness that comes out of understanding. Although I had always considered myself a patient person, my central failing in the story just told was my lack of that admirable quality. And one sense of *irony,* according to the same authority, is incongruity between what might be expected and what actually occurs. What I expected and what actually occurred were incongruous for two long years. When my patience gave out and I expected little or nothing to result from our efforts, the fruits began to be harvested.

And the harvest continues. The transcripts, which seemed such an extravagance in 1974, are still a gold mine for John Dore and his students; Peter Kranz, working without compensation, has nearly finished the machine-readable versions of all our naturalistic data. The experiments I wanted, which seemed so difficult to conduct on three-year-olds, were finally conducted (and many are still being analyzed) by Joyce Weil and Elsa Bartlett; both have found that minilongitudinal studies really can provide important information that is unobtainable from cross-sectional studies. The study of how children learn individual words, which once seemed so impossible, is now a promising area for future research, thanks to Sue Carey and Elsa Bartlett. Keith Stenning, who had no time for child language in 1974, finally became interested enough to conduct an experiment on children's memory for sentences. Even the computer, which failed so dismally as an input device, is now being used by Bob Jarvella for studies of reading comprehension. And Mike Cole is beginning to use the playroom and television equipment to study conversations among schoolchildren who, for a while, are allowed to enjoy themselves and become experts at socially valued activities like cooking or running a greenhouse.

In short, the funds made available by The Grant Foundation were not wasted after all, although their utilization did not develop in precisely the way we expected when we asked for them. The story has a happy ending.

I think it also has a moral, at least for me. Very simply: you should not expect scientific results of any value to grow overnight. They are not like commodities on store shelves that you can pay for and take home. They are not even like custom-tailored suits that you can order to your specifications and expect to receive on schedule. I am not sure what they are like. Gambles, perhaps, with unexpected payoffs.

I began writing this account with an uncomfortable feeling that I had not made good on my implicit commitment to The Grant Foundation, that the two years of the kiddie lab had been a failure. As I relived it during the writing, however, my perspective changed. In fact, as I now realize, the group accomplished a great deal; a modest summary might be that we achieved a much more informed state of ignorance. But now I am even more chagrined on a different score—my lack of patience. I *knew* that science grows organically in unpredictable ways over relatively long periods of time. I myself had said it dozens of times. Why did I expect the kiddie lab to be different? I should have expected the integration of experimental methods in a naturalistic context to be an especially gradual and deliberate achievement. And studies of development are the last places from which one should expect to achive quick results. It embarrasses me that, in spite of a dozen reasons not to, I fell into exactly the frame of mind that I had criticized in others.

During the period following World War II, the scientific and technological enterprise of the United States grew rapidly in size and appetite until it eventually became clear that not every project of intrinsic merit could be supported. Choices became increasingly necessary, and the basis for making those choices had to reflect the needs of the society that was paying the bill. In order to insure that the large sums being invested in science and technology should yield returns likely to promote the public welfare, scientists and engineers have been increasingly pressed to consider, explain, and where possible predict the practical consequences of the work they propose to do.

Thus, in recent years the goals of science and technology have become a matter of considerable public interest. Given a goal that is worth achieving, intelligent decisions can be made among alternative proposals for achieving it. This approach works reasonably well for most technological projects, but it creates problems for scientists. It is the essence of science that it explores the unknown, which introduces an element of unpredictability that is difficult to incorporate in any rational system of planning. Scientific goals can be set in advance only in the most general terms. Scientists who want an opportunity to mess around in some area that looks promising have difficulty stating well-defined goals. Yet under the pressure of public policy they have tried.

In the social and behavioral sciences, the kinds of goals people can understand have to do with better housing, racial integration, prevention and cure of disease, better education, environmental protection, and so on. These are very real problems, but they are not scientific problems. The most scientists can hope to do is to make more powerful tools available to ameliorate such problems. It takes time to put those tools to work, but the time spans during which the public is willing to wait are often unrealistically short. Thus, there is conflict between the public's reasonable expectation that science should do good and the scientist's own passion to do well the work to which his life is dedicated. I have repeatedly deplored the effects on scientific research and education caused by increasing public impatience with the slow and unpredictable course of scientific advances.

But how easy it is to fall into that impatient frame of mind! To blame my own impatience on the spirit of the times would be a lame and undignified excuse. I simply made a mistake. I can do little more now than apologize to my colleagues who suffered from it and admit that the public's attitude toward science is more seductive than I had realized.

If science develops in slow and unpredictable ways, so do scientists. Or are those just two ways to say the same thing? Elsa Bartlett, who seemed to me so intuitive during Year One, has grown into a committed and productive scientist. John Dore has discovered himself and what he has to contribute to the study of child language. Joyce Weil has integrated her teaching and research, to the benefit of both, and learned that administrative skill and scientific creativity are not incompatible. Personally, I not only survived to fight again another day—I am wiser (and not much sadder) about my own strengths and weaknesses in collaborative research. And all of us know a great deal more about children and how to study them.

I like to think that there are few errors, either of commision or omission, that the natural processes of learning cannot digest and grow on—if only you are lucky enough to remain a spontaneous apprentice to life.

Girl (on play telephone):   David!
Boy (not picking up other phone):   I'm not home.
Girl: When you'll be back?
Boy: I'm not here already.
Girl: But WHEN YOU'LL BE BACK?
Boy: Don't you know if I'm gone already, I went BE-
FORE so I can't talk to you!

Postscript

On rereading this story I see that I have frequently accentuated the negative. Perhaps that is how I am—born a martini behind everybody else. This tendency to see what is wrong more clearly than I see what is right makes me sound as though I have a very dreary outlook on life —like the kind of person who, when shaken out of a sound slumber and asked "Yes or No?" automatically answers "No."

In truth, however, my life, even during the hectic years described, was not a pastiche of different shades of depression. I really am capable of enthusiasm. The fact that I am reluctant to trust all my enthusiasms does not mean that I never feel them.

I say, for example, that I finally closed my personal postgraduate School of Developmental Psychology when the kiddie lab closed. That is true—I did give up my personal ambition to become a developmental psychologist—but I tell it as if it were an admission of defeat. I could also have told it as if it had been a success—having accomplished what I set out to do, I turned to some of the many other things I need to learn. Which was it really—a failure or a success? It was both, of course. It was a failure because the plan to create a large and active laboratory doing research on child language had to be abandoned. But what I learned while the kiddie lab was running has enriched my understanding of both children and language; never again will I think about psychological processes without considering their developmental aspects. In that respect, it was a success. Indeed, the writing of this account is tangible evidence that I have not lost interest in the problems we studied.

I also describe various technical problems we did not anticipate, and mistakes that we would not make again. I could easily have subordinated the mistakes to what we learned from them. That would have been a much more positive account, a recipe for creating a successful research program.

Take our problems of data management. If we had to do the project over again, knowing what we know now, how would we proceed? Now, of course, we know exactly what would have to be done, step by step. Instructions for all the different tasks could be written out in detail; criteria for selecting people with a talent for transcription would be established; mechanical details (like separate recorders for separate voices) would be incorporated from the beginning; the computer programming would be available and data processing would be possible while data collection was continuing.

We are in a special position, of course, as the result of two years of work, but we will not do the project over again because we now have a large and valuable corpus of child utterances of the kind we set out to collect. But those starting from scratch could profit from our experience. What is involved can be inferred from our experience, and some of the major pitfalls to be avoided are clearly posted in the preceding pages. That is a positive contribution, in spite of my moaning about the various pits we had to climb out of.

Or take our problems of conducting minilongitudinal studies of vocabulary growth. Many old hands at this kind of research would probably think we were re-inventing the wheel; I do describe it as if we were unbelievably naive at first. I could just as easily have emphasized with pride the beautiful chromium wheel that Sue and Elsa finally produced, as if we knew all along where we were going. But candor requires me to admit that I, at least, really was pretty naive at first—this is honest, and has the expository advantage of enabling me to take the reader along with me while I learn how this particular kind of wheel is made. But it does, once again, accentuate our difficulties more than our accomplishments.

I also apologize profusely for not becoming more directly involved in the day-to-day work of the kiddie lab. The apologies are necessary—I did not do everything I promised, and I am sorry. But I am not sorry about what I did instead. The bulk of my time and attention went into a writing project that I saw as being closely related to the work in the kiddie lab. Phil Johnson-Laird and I completed a splendid and important book that I have no intention of apologizing for. If these years of my life are remembered for anything, I hope it will be as the years we wrote *Language and Perception*, not as the years I spent in despondency about child language. If I wanted to tell the story of that book, I could give a very different impression of my state of mind at the time.

I do say a bit about the book, but only enough (I hope) to make the present tale intelligible. I do not try to explain *why* I think finishing it was more important than pursuing my developmental education. The reason is that I think psychological studies of language presently stand in much greater need of better theoretical formulations than of more empirical data. Language is, in general, something we know far more about than we understand, and this disparity between knowing how to speak and understanding how we speak can only be reduced by increasing our understanding—which I take to mean, by formulating better theories. Writing the book took longer than we expected (I apologize profusely for misestimating that, too); but, given the choice again, I would make the same decision today that I made then.

I do find depressing the short supply of theories adequate to support more insightful experimentation, but this depression is not mine alone. I have heard it expressed by several colleagues whose opinions I value. It is simply a fact: human languages are so complicated that good theories are hard to formulate. Without good theories, of course, only luck can guide us to make significant observations in the field or laboratory. But the depression I feel on this score is a deep depression, beyond anesthesia, and not to be confused with any unhappiness I felt about events transpiring in the kiddie lab.

Nobody ever promised us that science would be easy. Human beings and human communication did not evolve for the convenience of research workers. It is hard, slow work; only a saint would never complain. But it does accumulate, and even in two short years we made real progress. I want the reader to understand how difficult the work is, but I hope my emphasis on the difficulties will not obscure the real joy and pride we all felt in what was accomplished.

A friendly critic advised me that my story read like one of those Russian novels in which you are always confused about the cast of characters. I am not free to exercise a novelist's prerogative of reducing the number of people who figure in my narrative, for it would be misleading to suggest that research is conducted by three of four individuals in social isolation. However I thought I could lighten the load on the reader's memory by including (in alphabetical order) the following personal and biographical notes on some of the people who were working in my lab at the time.

MARK ALTOM. Mark was a graduate student in Bill Estes's lab, but he maintained an affiliation with my lab as well. He attended our lab meetings regularly, gave me a number of valuable criticisms of The Book, tried to use our children for a study of color discrimination in Year One, and collaborated with Joyce Weil in a study of spatial vs. temporal ordering of events in Year Two.

MARY JO ALTOM. During Year One Mary Jo performed a variety of jobs for us, including such things as helping Peter Kranz keep track of the status of all transcriptions. During Year Two she was the perfect assistant for Joyce Weil. She had a mother's intuition about three-year-olds, was familiar with the operation of the lab during Year One, had learned the rudiments of running the computer from Mark and Peter, was bright enough to understand Joyce's research plans and to learn how to test children objectively, and, above all, was reliable and could be there when Joyce could not.

ELSA JAFFE BARTLETT. What more can I say here about Elsa? As they say in indexes, *passim,* for without her efforts in Year One there would have been no story to tell, and far fewer results to report without her efforts in Year Two. What does not come out in the preceding pages, however, is her considerable experience in a wide variety of educational enterprises. She was an active contributor to education and educational research for several years before she decided to pick up her doctoral degree from Harvard. At Harvard it was Courtney Cazden who introduced Elsa to research on language acquisition, which has since become her central intellectual addiction.

SUSAN CAREY. Sue was a member of the Psychology Department at the Massachusetts Institute of Technology. Although I had known her since she was an undergraduate at Radcliffe, it was Elsa Bartlett who persuaded Sue to become a regular visitor during Year Two. Her broad knowledge of research on cognitive development expanded our horizons significantly. She was particularly helpful to Elsa, but what I appreciated most were her comments on The Book. She assigned herself the task of reading the pile of manuscript that Phil Johnson-Laird and I had accumulated, and almost every visit left me grateful for the ideas, comments, and corrections that she contributed to it.

MADELEINE DOBRINER. Just across the street from the Rockefeller University is the William Woodward Jr. Nursery School, where we have gone repeatedly to find an intelligent and cooperative staff who would help us satisfy our curiosity about the ways and wiles of young children. For three years before Elsa enticed her away, Madeleine had been a teacher at Woodward. The College of New Rochelle had given her a B.A. in art, but all of her work experience had been in nursery schools. She devised an excellent curriculum to educate our children when research problems were lacking, and collaborated enthusiastically when research problems were proposed. Eliciting spontaneous speech from children on particular topics is a difficult and imperfect art, but she was never at a loss for natural ways to incorporate a research goal into classroom activities. The kiddie lab exploited her talents in new ways that stimulated her interest in child language and thought, and added new dimensions to her skills as an early childhood teacher. When the playroom closed she stayed on for a while to edit the transcripts and to write an excellent summary of her two years of work with us.

JOHN DORE. It was reading Noam Chomsky's *Syntactic Structures* that convinced John he wanted to be a linguist, and somewhere along the way to that goal he read John Searle's *Speech Acts.* His academic home in New York is the English Department of Baruch College, where he taught while working for his doctoral degree in linguistics at the City University of New York, received in 1973, and where he is now a faculty member.

ROBERT JARVELLA. Bob took his Ph.D. in psycholinguistics at Michigan with an intriguing thesis in which he demonstrated that clause boundaries determine the amount of text a listener will hold in immediate memory while trying to understand spoken prose. He had spent 1970–71 with me at the Institute for Advanced Study before going to Case-Western Reserve in 1971. When I decided to get my laboratory back together, I called Bob and asked whether he would like to join me. Since he had personal reasons for wanting to be in New York, I was able to attract him. In Cleveland he had done some work with child language, which was an added bonus for me, but the important thing was that, with Bob aboard, I knew that the kind of research I had pursued for many years would be well represented while I went off in new directions.

PETER KRANZ. Peter was our computer guru, but his real interests are good food, good wine, time budgets, and a farm in Connecticut. As long as I could pay him he used part of the money for visits to France, from which he would return with recipes and cases of wine. When I could no longer pay him, he continued to work on our transcriptions and to help us bring the adventure to a documented conclusion.

DONNA KWILOSZ LYONS. At Clarke College Donna majored in psychology and planned on going to medical school. After marriage and a move from Chicago to New York she was working during the days and going to the New School in the evenings. In April 1973 she saw an ad in *The New York Times* for a secretary to a psychologist, applied, and landed the job. Her role in everything that transpired subsequently was far more important than the preceding pages would suggest. She is more an administrative assistant than a secretary, although she says she dislikes administering anything. In any case, without her skill in typing, The Book could never have been rewritten as many times as it was; without her mastery of the intricacies of Rockefeller University, nothing would have gotten built, bought, or borrowed; and without her eye on the budget sheets I could never have pretended to be running a laboratory.

KEITH STENNING. When I left Rockefeller to go to the Institute for Advanced Study in 1970, my laboratory at Rockefeller was disbanded. Mike Cole began using the space; Tom Bever accepted a professorship at Columbia; and my secretary took another job; two of my three graduate students transferred to W. K. Estes's laboratory of mathematical psychology. The third graduate student, Keith Stenning, was not interested in mathematical psychology. Keith had come from Oxford to work with me on the psychology of language; in my absence he worked on the psychology of language by himself. I saw him almost every week, but he had to hammer out his thesis topic on his own. He settled on a study of English articles (*a*, *the*) and quantifiers (*some*, *all*, *any*) and developed a detailed argument that their interpretation in ordinary use depends on general rules of discourse, of which grammatical rules are but a special case. It was a major effort, and after all he had gone through to formulate it, he was not about to give it up in order to work with children. He continued on his autonomous course, watched with mild amusement my interest in the kiddie lab (which he regarded as a temporary derangement on my part), and eventually completed a long and important thesis. Once the thesis was out of the way, however, he did become involved in a study of children's memory for sentences. Keith is presently Lecturer in Psychology at the University of Liverpool.

JOYCE WEIL. As a graduate student at the City University of New York, Joyce had major responsibility for a large longitudinal study of children in Harlem. After a Ph.D. thesis in which she analyzed the relation between children's conception of time and the language they use to express it, she took a staff position at the Russell Sage Foundation. But an interest in children tends to be addictive; when the opportunity arose, she moved to a research job at the Children's Television Workshop. And when the research side of television proved less glamorous than production, she returned to a university position. In recounting her contributions to the kiddie lab, especially during Year Two, I may have overemphasized the administrative skills she had picked up along the way—not because that was all she had to offer, but because that was what I needed most desperately.

YESHIVA GRADUATE STUDENTS. The kiddie lab provided an opportunity for some of Joyce Weil's students at the Ferkauf Graduate School of Humanities and Social Sciences, Yeshiva University, to gain practical experience in child research, and they provided us with skilled assistance in a variety of tasks. In addition to the intelligence tests given by students training to become school psychologists, several students in developmental psychology served as transcribers and typists for the video recordings. Merlyn Dolins, Alice Florance, Phyllis Goldstein, Joan Monaghan, Karen Sanazaro, Alina Shumsky, and Doris Stone deserve our special gratitude for the research they conducted in support of Joyce's longitudinal study of time language.

References

Brown, R. *A First Language: The Early Stages.* Cambridge, Mass.: Harvard University Press, 1973.

Bruner, J. S. *On Knowing: Essays for the Left Hand.* Cambridge, Mass.: Harvard University Press, 1962.

Clark, E. V. "On the Child's Acquisition of Antonyms in Two Semantic Fields," *Journal of Verbal Learning and Verbal Behavior,* 1972, 11, 750–758.

Clark, E. V. "What's in a Word? On the Child's Acquisition of Semantics in His First Language," T. E. Moore (ed.), *Cognitive Development and the Acquisition of Language.* New York: Academic Press, 1973.

Miller, G. A. *Language and Communication.* New York: Mc-Graw-Hill, 1951.

Miller, G. A., and P. N. Johnson-Laird. *Language and Perception.* Cambridge, Mass.: Harvard University Press, 1976.

Sacks, H. "On the Analysability of Stories by Children." In J. J. Gumperz and D. Hymes (eds.), *Directions in Sociolinguistics: the Ethnology of Communication.* New York: Holt, Rinehart and Winston, 1972.

Templin, M. C. *Certain Language Skills in Children: Their Development and Interrelationships.* Minneapolis: University of Minnesota Press, 1957.

Whitehead, A. N. *Introduction to Mathematics.* New York: Holt, 1939.

About the Author

George A. Miller received his Ph.D. in Psychology from Harvard University in 1946. His early research on the perception of speech led him to apply the mathematical theory of communication to the problem, but when the limitations of that theory for the description of human language became clear, he took up the study of grammar as a formal system and showed that perceptual processes are subject to the language user's implicit knowledge of the syntactic and semantic rules of his language. Interest in syntax eventually gave way to interest in semantics, and the desire to test some of his theoretical proposals about how people learn and remember the meanings of words led to the program of research described in this book.

Dr. Miller is Professor of Experimental Psychology at The Rockefeller University and Visiting Professor at Massachusetts Institute of Technology. He has served as president of the American Psychological Association, is a member of the National Academy of Sciences, and has published numerous articles and books on psychology, language, and communication.

About the Editor of This Series

Ruth Nanda Anshen, philosopher and editor, plans and edits *World Perspectives, Religious Perspectives, Perspectives in Humanism, Credo Perspectives, The Science of Culture Series,* and *The Tree of Life* series. She also writes and lectures on the relationship of knowledge to the nature and meaning of man and his existence. She is the author of *The Reality of the Devil: Evil in Man,* a study in the phenomenology of evil. Dr. Anshen is Chairman of the Columbia University Seminar on The Nature of Man, a member of the International Philosophical Society, The History of Science Society and the American Philosophical Association.